Justin GUITAR
Note Reading for Guitarists

Written, compiled and arranged by Justin Sandercoe and Dario Cortese.
Edited by Toby Knowles.
Designed by Fresh Lemon Australia.
Cover photographs by Nick Delaney.
Photo of Dario Cortese by Tina Korhonen.

ISBN: 978-1-78558-369-8

www.justinguitar.com

Visit Hal Leonard Online at
www.halleonard.com

World headquarters, contact:
Hal Leonard
7777 West Bluemound Road
Milwaukee, WI 53213
Email: info@halleonard.com

In Europe, contact:
Hal Leonard Europe Limited
1 Red Place
London, W1K 6PL
Email: info@halleonardeurope.com

In Australia, contact:
Hal Leonard Australia Pty. Ltd.
4 Lentara Court
Cheltenham, Victoria, 3192 Australia
Email: info@halleonard.com.au

Justin GUITAR
Note Reading for Guitarists

Justin Sandercoe & Dario Cortese

Table of contents

Introduction 6

Glossary and notation terms 11

String 1

01 - Notes on string 1 (thin E string) 14

02 - Adding basic rhythm 16

03 - Adding rests 18

String 2

04 - Notes on string 2 (B string) 20

05 - Combining notes on strings 1 and 2 22

06 - Notes on strings 1 and 2 with rhythms 24

07 - Notes on strings 1 and 2 with rhythms and rests 26

08 - Double-stops on strings 1 and 2 28

String 3

09 - Notes on string 3 (G string) 30

10 - Notes on strings 1, 2 and 3 32

11 - Notes on strings 1, 2 and 3 with rhythms 34

12 - Notes on strings 1, 2 and 3 with rhythms and rests 36

13 - Strings 1, 2 and 3 with double-stops 36

14 - Your first duet 39

15 - Introducing $\frac{3}{4}$ time 42

16 - $\frac{3}{4}$ Study 44

String 4

17 - Notes on string 4 (D string) 46

18 - Notes on the thinnest four strings 48

19 - Notes on the thinnest four strings with rhythms 50

20 - Notes on the thinnest four strings with rhythms and rests 52

21 - Thinnest four strings with double-stops 54

22 - Thinnest four strings with small chords 56

23 - Introducing eighth-notes 58

String 5

24 - Notes on string 5 (A string) 60

25 - Notes on the thinnest five strings 62

26 - Thinnest five strings with rhythms 62

27 - Thinnest five strings with rhythms and rests 65

28 - Thinnest five strings with double-stops 65

29 - Thinnest five strings with chords 68

30 - Duet #2 68

31 - Introducing $\frac{2}{4}$ 72

String 6

32 - Notes on the thickest E string 74

33 - Ledger lines 76

34 - Notes on all six strings! 78

35 - All six strings with rhythms 78

36 - All six strings with rhythms and rests 78

37 - All six strings with double-stops 82

38 - All six strings with chords 84

39 - Random note study #1 86

Accidentals

40 - Accidentals 88

41 - Accidentals on the thinnest three strings 90

42 - Accidentals on all strings 92

43 - Accidentals on all strings with rhythm 94

44 - All strings with accidentals, rhythms and rests 96

45 - Accidentals, rhythms, rests and double-stops 98

46 - Chords and accidentals 100

47 - Duet #2 100

More rhythms

48 - Introduction to two voices 104

49 - Introduction to syncopation 106

50 - Eighth-note rests 108

51 - Ties 110

52 - Dots 112

53 - Introducing $\frac{6}{8}$ time 114

54 - $\frac{6}{8}$ study 116

Scale studies

55 - G major scale key study 118

56 - F major scale key study 120

57 - D major scale key study 122

58 - A major scale key study 124

59 - Random note studies 126

Repertoire

Introduction 128

27 easy pieces 131

 Introduction

Should you learn to read notation?

An important question before starting any journey is: why you are making it! Learning to read notation is not for everyone and for the hobby guitar player, reading guitar TAB is often far better because it shows where to play the note—which is one of the great challenges when reading notation. And there are many examples of professional musicians (including some of the finest guitar players of all time) who don't read music at all! So why would you want to put in the effort to learn to read the dots?

Learning how to read music is very similar to learning how to read other languages. Acquiring the skill allows us to read great books, magazines and newspapers. It allows us to expand our vocabulary of words, phrases and ideas. In addition, because reading and writing go hand in hand, it also allows us to better communicate our ideas to others. There are (unfortunately) many people in the world who cannot read or write but they can still communicate by speaking, often very effectively.

The same is true for reading music: it allows us to access a vast collection of written music without the need to 'hear it first'. This is true not just for music written for guitar but also music written for other instruments too. And because reading music and writing music are related it also makes communicating our ideas to other musicians very quick and easy.

There are many positive side effects of learning how to read notation.

The first noticeable side effect is the improvement of our fretboard knowledge. Because reading requires the ability to quickly find the notes on the guitar we start becoming aware of what we are actually playing and this has a dramatic effect on areas such as improvising and composition. (TAB does not tell us what the notes are, just where to play them!)

Reading encourages the understanding of harmony—because we become aware of the notes we play and that naturally draws us to understand more about the relationship between notes and chords.

Another common side effect is rhythmic accuracy because we can identify very clearly what a rhythm is, we can also identify what is not. This is one of the most noticeable (and very positive) side effects we have seen in students that learn to read notation.

Under which circumstances should you start reading music? The only situation where you really must learn how to read music is if you want to become a professional guitarist. And this is simply because reading music maximises your opportunity for employment.

Obviously there are many other situations where reading can be essential or a big help.

If you want to play classical guitar it is essential that you learn how to read. There are some books with notation and TAB but for the most part classical repertoire is written in notation.

If you want to play in a band, learning how to read can seriously minimise the time needed to learn a song (you can write your own charts, which will help you memorise the notes and arrangement, and you can use as a cheat while rehearsing!) and it makes communicating ideas with other people in your band a lot easier. Try to learn 30 songs in a week and you'll get what we mean.

If you are a music student then we highly recommend that you learn to read music.

However, with the proliferation of guitar TAB on the internet there are fewer people needing to read notation. If you are a hobby guitar player that likes playing songs, strumming and just having fun and are not yet interested in working professionally or playing in a band or classical music then reading notation may not be for you! So we strongly recommend that you think about the reason for learning before you start and start when you need to—not just because you think you 'should'—it is possible to become a great guitar player without learning to read!

Making the most of this book

In creating this book, we wanted to create a smooth and easy path into reading notation for guitar players. It can be a daunting task so we have tried to break it down as much as possible to make the progression as easy as possible from having no experience to being able to read confidently in open position (the first 5 frets).

We have done this by introducing one string at a time and gradually introducing other aspects such as rhythms and rests slowly as you progress.

Practice

There is no substitute for doing it and the hours you put into reading will directly correlate with how quickly you become a fluent reader. If you can find time to work on your reading each practice session you will notice faster and more solid progress.

Repetition is very important but you need to try to avoid 'learning' the reading studies. They're not songs or melodies—they're studies. One way to help combat this problem is to read the exercises backwards (where possible) or reading alternate lines. Just keeping in mind that you are not to memorise the exercises will probably help.

The four steps

It can be very helpful to understand the four elements that occur when reading and also to realise that the first three of them can be worked on independently. For many people it's a nice way to start because it makes the steps as simple as possible.

1. **Recognising the notes on the stave**
   Before you play a note you have to read the note and know what it is—what is the note name? This can be worked on without your guitar—you can use any notation you have, for any instrument. You can do it anywhere it's safe to read—just look at the notation and name the notes you see!

2. **Recognising the rhythm of the notes**
   Music is the combination of rhythm and melody so it's obviously important to know the rhythm of the notes you should play. Again you can work on this using any sheet music and work on it anywhere. Just look at the notation and tap out the rhythm.

3. **Knowing where the notes are found on the guitar neck**
   This area can be challenging on the guitar because almost every note on the guitar can be played in more than one place on the neck—however, in this book we are just dealing with notes in the open position—that is the first 5 frets, so we'll be presenting each note in only one place and we'll deal with moving positions in a later volume when you're comfortable in open position.

4. **Developing the sight reading 'flow'**
   The final step is learning to Sight Read, which is essentially 'playing on sight'. This process is best developed SLOWLY so that you can get it right. There is little benefit from practising sloppy playing. When sight reading, start slowly enough that you can play well without stopping.

The panic inducer (metronome)

One thing we think can be very effective at the right time is using a metronome during your sight reading practice. Because it will stop you from pausing, it can induce a kind of panic which occurs in the 'real world' and is something that can be beneficial even at the early stages—but make sure of two things:

- Set the tempo slow enough for you to be able to play the study (or song) easily and only speed up when you can confidently play all the way through without mistakes.

- If you do 'fall off' then try to keep the rhythm by following the music with your eyes and get back on at the right place—usually it's easiest to start again at the start of the next bar. This is likely to take a lot of practice but should be the goal for most people. After some experience you will find that you know your place in the bar without having to follow along with your eyes, which will make it easier to come back in in the right place. If you aspire to play a 'reading gig' at any point then the ability to come back in the right place is essential!

British vs. American terms

Guitarists and pop/rock musicians tend to use 'American' terms to describe different note lengths, and that is what we've used in this book too.

If you're familiar with the more traditional terms, used prevalently in the United Kingdom, we have included both in the chart below so you can learn either as you wish. If you are studying music it would be a great idea to ask your teacher which they want you to learn but they are pretty simple and learning both is the best option.

Note	UK	US
o	Semibreve	Whole Note
♩	Minim	Half-Note
♩	Crotchet	Quarter-Note
♪	Quaver	Eighth-Note
♪	Semiquaver	Sixteenth-Note

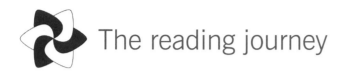

The reading journey

Justin's reading journey

I started playing guitar when I was very young and did my first gig at 12 years old and by the time I was 17 I was playing four or more gigs a week and was teaching at least 20 students every week. But I could not read music at all—I had been learning almost everything I knew by ear (I did have some private lessons too, though not consistently!).

My father insisted that I go to university (get a real job!) and a compromise was reached by going to a music school—the only option in my town was The Tasmanian Conservatorium of Music which at the time was a classical only school. I went to meet the head guitar teacher for a chat and he told me that while there was no doubt I could play well enough, I had to be able to read too, and that there was no way I would be accepted to the school without reasonable sight reading skills. But he was a rock guy at heart, so he gave me a challenge and gave me Andre Segovia's edition of the Fernando Sor Study IX and said that if I could figure it out and come and play it in a month he'd accept my determination to read and let me in. Study IX looks like a fly had diarrhoea all over the page, very scary indeed, but I put my head down and figured it out and learned a lot about reading in the process. And after a pretty rough audition fumbling through a few classical pieces I was accepted.

I spent two years studying classical guitar by day and gigging with rock and funk covers bands by night before moving to London to study at The Guitar Institute in London. There I learned more about reading charts in a jazz and pop context and after my Diploma there I took a job playing in a holiday camp band where I was reading pop music charts on sight for different artists, six nights a week. Being in a 'pickup band' forced me to step up my game big time. I made plenty of mistakes but tried to learn from each one and was doing alright after six months. I only lasted about nine months there before moving back to London to join another band. Since then I've not done a lot of reading gigs and to be honest my sight reading is getting pretty rusty but I still enjoy playing classical guitar as a kind of 'recreational study' and of course I read and write music for my books and website lessons.

Dario's reading journey

I started playing guitar when I was 11 and I knew pretty much straight away that I wanted to do it for a living. I was inspired by lots of different types of musicians: from famous guitarists to session and orchestra musicians—the people who are mostly unknown to the wider audience. I was fascinated by written music from the start. I wanted to understand the language that musicians were able to read so I taught myself how to do it. I remember playing around with my Atari computer and using Cubase's grid to try to figure out note lengths! It was a trial and error process until things sounded right.

Initially it was difficult to get my dream accepted by my parents, because like most parents, they wanted me to go for a much 'safer' career. Me being stubborn and determined I eventually won their trust and started having guitar lessons. My teacher didn't really check if I could read or not, he just 'assumed' I could and I managed to go along with it and he never found out! In the meantime, I started playing in bands and duos. Because there was so much music to remember I used to write myself charts to help me remember songs. I was about 15, doing four or five gigs a week and teaching privately. Also I got passionate about the piano, so I used to sit down and tried to read piano scores and this helped a lot more than I realised at that time. After that I went to a music school to get a qualification as a musician (part of the deal with my parents). Unfortunately, that didn't really help my reading because the class was aimed at guitarists who were just starting to read and I could already read basic stuff so I used to skip that class.

As soon as I moved to London I started teaching at The Guitar Institute (where Justin and I met) and almost immediately I started getting busier with sessions and gigs. At first I shied away from proper reading gigs, because although I could read reasonably well, I didn't feel I had enough experience. Although I wasn't really doing 'reading gigs' I was still practising reading so I felt that in those years my reading really improved.

But things stepped up a gear when I got involved in theatre. I had to learn very quickly how to read and interpret all kinds of part. And not just guitar parts! Often guitarists get asked to play mandolin, ukulele, banjo, and anything that has strings. On top of that I got used to following a conductor while reading and changing effects!

From there it became somehow easier. Once people know you can read you start getting more reading gigs which in turn make your reading better. Nowadays I get mostly reading gigs: from the work in the West End of London, the place where all the musicals are, to playing with bands and orchestras of all sizes. Somehow I still feel that my reading has a long way to go compared to some of the professionals I get to meet, but I also know that the only to way to improve is to actually keep doing it. It's a never-ending process!

Glossary and notation terms

Stave

The stave is the five lines (and four spaces) that we write notes on to represent pitches and rhythms in music.

Please be aware that in this book we are only looking at standard notation, not TAB notation.
The differences are explained below.

TAB notation is written on a six line stave—each line represents a string on the guitar, and for this reason the music can only be played on a guitar.

Standard notation uses a five line stave, and is much more versatile than TAB—the music can be played on many different instruments.

Treble clef

The treble clef is the squiggle that vaguely resembles a snail with an antenna on its back that you will find at the start of a stave (see the stave example above). This is the only 'clef' you will see in this book (and for nearly all guitar music) although there are other clefs for other instruments—e.g. the piano has two staves, one with a treble clef (normally for the right hand) and one with a bass clef (usually for the left hand).

Note heads and tails

The stave is where you write individual notes. The note heads (the round or 'eliptical' part of the note) in combination with the tail (or 'flag') will tell you how long a note lasts for. Here are some examples of the sort of noteheads that you'll see in this book.

Rests

A rest means silence, so stop any notes you are playing! Here are some examples of the rests that you'll find in this book.

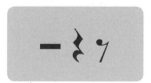

Ties

A 'tie' is a line that ties one note to another. So you'll play just one note, but you'll hold it for the combined duration of the two (or more) notes that are tied together.

Tempo

You'll often see a tempo or metronome mark at the start of the music to tell you how fast or slow it should be.

This may be an Italian word like 'Allegro' (meaning 'fast' or 'lively') or a more specific metronome mark. The metronome markings are written in BPM which stands for 'beats per minute'.

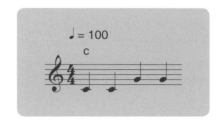

Time Signature

A time signature tells you how many beats you have in a bar.

The top number tells you the amount of beats and the bottom the value of the beat. For example $\frac{4}{4}$ time is 4 (top note) quarter-notes (bottom note is 4) in a bar. $\frac{6}{8}$ time will have 6 (top note) eighth-notes in a bar (bottom note is 8). In this book we're only looking at $\frac{4}{4}$, $\frac{3}{4}$ (3 quarter-notes in a bar), $\frac{2}{4}$ (2 quarter-notes in a bar) and $\frac{6}{8}$.

The top number tells you how many counts there are in a bar.

The bottom number tells you the value of each count.

Anacrusis

Sometimes you will find notes at the start of a piece that do not add to a whole bar. These are an 'anacrusis' and are often 3 or 4 notes that 'lead in' to the piece.

In pop and jazz charts they're sometimes referred to as 'pick up notes'. An example is the first three notes of 'Johnny B. Goode'.

Key Signature

The key signature tells you the key you are in by indicating which notes are sharp of flat in the key.

Every key (except C major) has a different number of sharps of flats in it so if you know your music theory, it's easy to tell the key just from the key signature. The important thing to remember is that if a note if shown as a sharp of flat in the key signature, every time you see that note in the music you will play the relevant sharp or flat.

For example, if you see a ♯ on the top line (the note F), you will play F♯ every time you see an F note in the music, unless it is cancelled by a natural sign (♮). When we see a sharp or flat symbol that is not in the key signature, the note is described as an **accidental**.

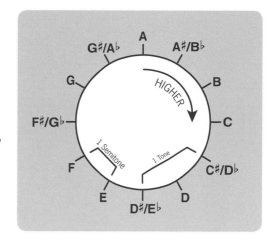

Sharps and flats

When we first learn note names, we learn the natural notes, which are labelled A, B, C, D, E, F, G (and happen to be the white notes on the piano). However, there are several extra pitches in between these notes, which are called sharps or flats, depending on the key of the piece.

Sharps are a semitone (half-step) higher, and flats are a semitone lower. Look at the table to see where the sharps and flats are located.

Octaves

Each pitch can be played in a number of different octaves, meaning that there are numerous higher or lower octave versions of the same note.

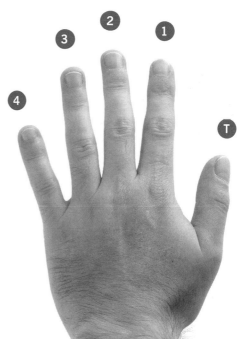

Syncopation

The definition is 'a temporary displacement of the regular accent in music caused by stressing a weak beat'—in the context of this book it means emphasising notes on the 'ands' and not on the strong beats (the numbers 1, 2, 3, 4), which changes the flow of the music.

Fingering

You'll see quite a few references to fingering in this book (e.g. 'play this note with finger 2'). This is referring to your fretting-hand fingers, which follow the pattern shown in this diagram:

Notation example

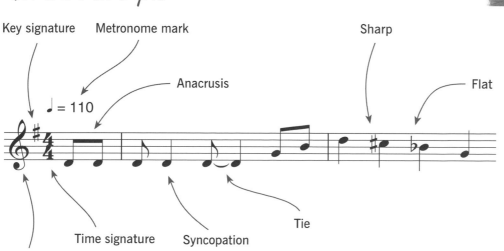

STRING 1

STRING 2

STRING 3

STRING 4

STRING 5

STRING 6

ACCIDENTALS

MORE RHYTHMS

SCALE STUDIES

REPERTOIRE

STEP 01 — Notes on string 1 (thin E string)

**We're going to start off by taking it very easy, using just three notes.
They are all found on the thinnest string.**

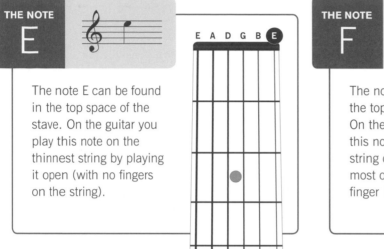

THE NOTE E

The note E can be found in the top space of the stave. On the guitar you play this note on the thinnest string by playing it open (with no fingers on the string).

THE NOTE F

The note F is found on the top line of the stave. On the guitar you play this note on the thinnest string on fret 1. This is most often played with finger 1.

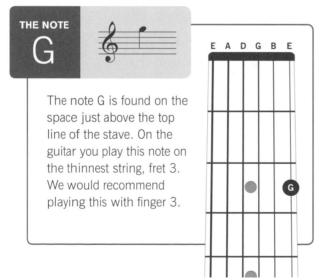

THE NOTE G

The note G is found on the space just above the top line of the stave. On the guitar you play this note on the thinnest string, fret 3. We would recommend playing this with finger 3.

Consistent fingering

One thing you might find helps is using consistent fingering. If a note is on fret 1 then use finger 1; if a note is on fret 2 then use finger 2, etc. In the 'real world' you will likely use whichever finger is closest to the note you want to play. However, it can be helpful to have a pattern to rely on whilst learning.

In this first exercise, the rhythm consists of even quarter-notes (four notes to the bar). At first you will likely find it hard to keep the rhythm steady. Once you become familiar with the notes, try to keep the rhythm as consistent as you can.

Start by counting out loud as you go (1, 2, 3, 4, 1, 2...). Although it might sound like a silly thing to do, vocalizing the rhythm is actually quite important. It helps internalizing the rhythm and developing a connection between us and the guitar. Eventually we want to 'feel' every beat and 'feel' the unity between hitting the guitar in time and counting.

Using a metronome will step it up a gear, so we recommend starting out without one. Only start using the metronome when you can play all the way through without stopping. If you've never used a metronome before, start at 60 bpm. Before you start, listen to it and count out loud with it for about 10–20 seconds. Make sure that the counting and the metronome are perfectly synchronised, not a second before or after. As you're counting, imagine how the piece will sound. Once you can do that playing along with it will be a lot easier.

STRING 1

STRING 2

STRING 3

STRING 4

STRING 5

STRING 6

ACCIDENTALS

MORE RHYTHMS

SCALE STUDIES

REPERTOIRE

EXERCISE 01 Notes on string 1 (thin E string)

STRING 1

STRING 2

STRING 3

STRING 4

STRING 5

STRING 6

ACCIDENTALS

MORE RHYTHMS

SCALE STUDIES

REPERTOIRE

STEP
02 Adding basic rhythm

Note reading can get boring very quickly unless we add in some rhythm. Obviously learning to read rhythm is part of the deal when learning to read music. In fact, it's a big part of learning how to read music. In this step we're going to introduce two new rhythmic values.

$\frac{4}{4}$ time

Most of this book is in the time signature of $\frac{4}{4}$ which means that each bar (also known as a measure) will contain four beats. We are sure that most of you will have heard people count to four when starting off a song. This is because $\frac{4}{4}$ time is the most common time signature in popular music.

Quarter-notes

The notes we saw in Exercise 1 were all 'quarter-notes' (also called 'crotchets'), which are worth 1 beat each. This is why you saw four of them in each bar in Exercise 1.

Note pyramid

You might find that this pyramid helps to visualise different rhythms. In one bar of $\frac{4}{4}$ time, we could fit either four quarter-notes, two half-notes, one whole note or a combination of one half-note and two quarter-notes. We will be adding more divisions of the beat later but it's always better to start simple and get confident with the basics first.

One whole note (semibreve)

Two half-notes (minims)

Four quarter-notes (crotchets)

Eight eight-notes (quavers)

Sixteen sixteenth-notes (semiquavers)

Half-notes

A note that is held for exactly twice as long as a quarter-note is called a half-note (also called 'minim'). Two quarters make a half, right? These look very similar to quarter-notes but the head of the note is hollow.

Whole notes

A note held twice as long as a half-note is called a whole note (also called 'semibreve')—two halves make a whole! They last for a whole bar in $\frac{4}{4}$ time, so they are said to be worth four beats. They look similar to half-notes but the stem is removed, so only the hollow note head remains.

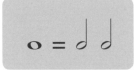

Exercises

Remember that it can be very helpful to look at the rhythm separately from the notes, especially when learning or encountering a particularly hard rhythmic section later on. It's a good idea to try tapping out the rhythm of the exercise before starting to play the notes. Only when you are confident with the rhythm should you start playing the notes and the rhythm together. When you tap the notes, be aware that you are playing where the note starts but not where it finishes.

STRING 1

STRING 2

STRING 3

STRING 4

STRING 5

STRING 6

ACCIDENTALS

MORE RHYTHMS

SCALE STUDIES

REPERTOIRE

EXERCISE 02 *Notes on string 1 with rhythms*

STRING 1
STRING 2
STRING 3
STRING 4
STRING 5
STRING 6
ACCIDENTALS
MORE RHYTHMS
SCALE STUDIES
REPERTOIRE

STEP 03 | Adding rests

Without silence, music would become very boring. So, now you understand the basics of rhythm, we will also look at the equivalent rests. Make sure that you mute the instrument when you encounter a rest.

It's worth noting at this point that, as soon as we include rests, we need to start thinking about when notes end rather than just when they start. So, as well as being 'silence in its own right', the rest helps us define the length of the previous note. The importance of this will become clearer as you play through the examples, but try to stay aware of note lengths—they're a big deal!

Quarter-note rest

'Quarter-note rests' (also called 'crotchet rests') have a very cool looking symbol that looks much like a C with a sloped hat on. You can also look at it as a number two on top of a C! You shouldn't have too many problems recognising it as it's got a pretty unique look within music notation. It is worth one beat.

Rest pyramid

Just like we saw the note pyramid in the previous lesson, here it is again but with rests!

One whole note rest (semibreve rest)

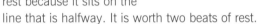

Two half-note rests (minims rests)

Four quarter-note rests (crotchet rests)

Eight eighth-note rests (quaver rests)

𝄾 𝄾 𝄾 𝄾 𝄾 𝄾 𝄾 𝄾

Sixteen sixteenth-note rests (semiquaver rests)

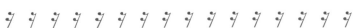

Half-note rest

A half-note rest is written as a long rectangle on top of the middle line of the stave. You can remember it's a half-note rest because it sits on the line that is halfway. It is worth two beats of rest.

Whole note rest

A whole note rest looks very similar to the half-note rest but hangs from the second highest line of the stave. You might find it helpful to remember it's a whole note rest because it's 'holding on' to the line—otherwise it would fall off!

Counting

It can be very helpful to whisper rests while counting along. It helps 'feeling' the length of the rest. It's oft-debated

as to whether counting rhythm while you read is a good idea or not but 'feeling' the rests is essential. Personally, we find it very helpful: learning to speak rhythms out loud helps a great deal with tricky passages. For instance, in the rhythm above we would 'whisper' the 3.

Justin GUITAR

STRING 1
STRING 2
STRING 3
STRING 4
STRING 5
STRING 6
ACCIDENTALS
MORE RHYTHMS
SCALE STUDIES
REPERTOIRE

EXERCISE 03 *Notes on string 1 with rhythms and rests*

STRING 1
STRING 2
STRING 3
STRING 4
STRING 5
STRING 6
ACCIDENTALS
MORE RHYTHMS
SCALE STUDIES
REPERTOIRE

STEP 04

Notes on string 2 (B string)

Now you know some notes and basic rhythms, we need to start expanding both. We'll be starting by expanding the notes you know. We're now looking at the notes in the open position on string 2, the B string.

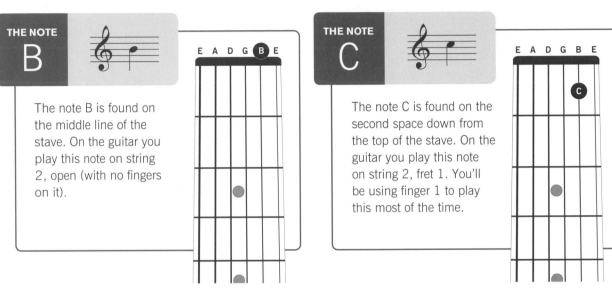

THE NOTE B

The note B is found on the middle line of the stave. On the guitar you play this note on string 2, open (with no fingers on it).

THE NOTE C

The note C is found on the second space down from the top of the stave. On the guitar you play this note on string 2, fret 1. You'll be using finger 1 to play this most of the time.

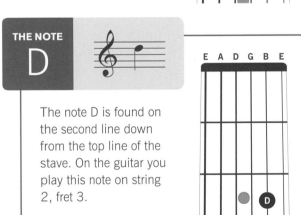

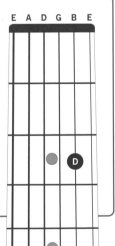

THE NOTE D

The note D is found on the second line down from the top line of the stave. On the guitar you play this note on string 2, fret 3.

Tip...

You might find it fun to read some of the exercises backwards too. There's no harm in exploring ideas in this way. Once you 'recognise the pattern' the exercise becomes less effective. Make sure to experiment to keep the music sounding as fresh as you can!

Exercise

Note that the following exercise is just the notes with no rhythms added. The exercise is really just about teaching you to recognise the notes as best you can.

Going through whilst naming the notes (without playing your guitar or even having it in your hands) can be a great way to really learn the notes on the page. Then you can start to play it on the guitar, making sure you keep the rhythm simple and accurate.

JustinGUITAR

STRING 1
STRING 2
STRING 3
STRING 4
STRING 5
STRING 6
ACCIDENTALS
MORE RHYTHMS
SCALE STUDIES
REPERTOIRE

EXERCISE 04

Notes on string 2 (B string)

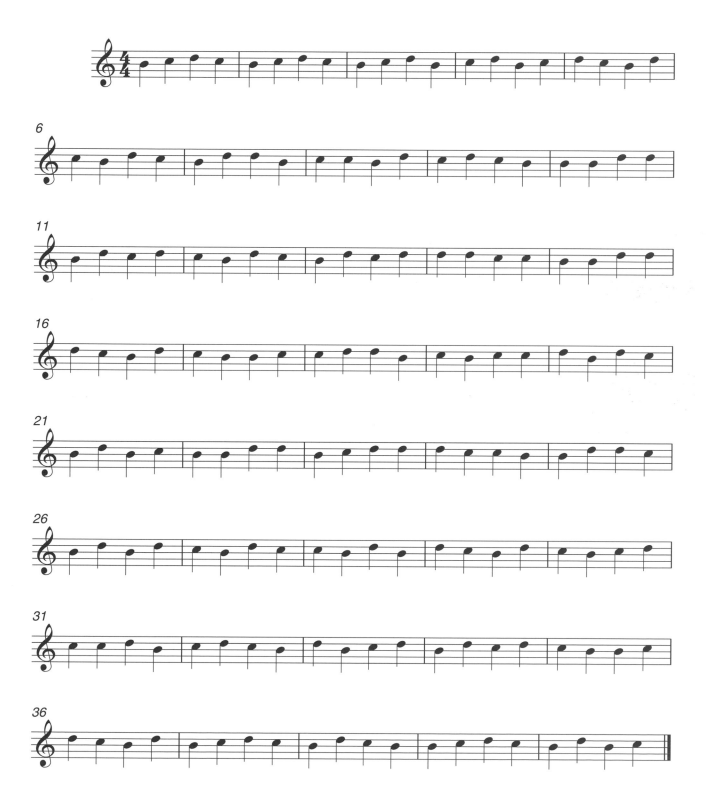

STRING 1

STRING 2

STRING 3

STRING 4

STRING 5

STRING 6

ACCIDENTALS

MORE RHYTHMS

SCALE STUDIES

REPERTOIRE

STEP 05 Combining notes on strings 1 and 2

You know six notes now and it's very important that you get them into your memory as soon as you can. It's no good having to refer to a chart—they really need to be memorised, so that you can recognise them in an instant.

The best way to work on memorising the notes is to play through the exercises as often as you can. Play them forwards and backwards or play every other line—mix things up as much as possible to force yourself to keep reading the notes!

There are two common devices that are very useful to remember the notes on the stave.

Every good boy

The phrase people use to remember the notes on the lines is:

Every   Good   Boy   Deserves   Fruit

The first letter of each word tells you the names of the notes on the lines of the stave.
The spaces are a little easier as they spell the word FACE.

F   A   C   E

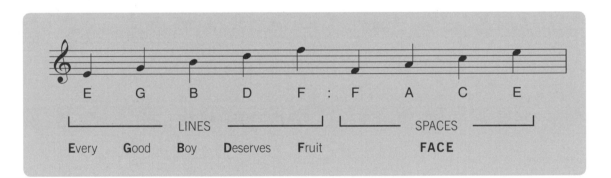

You are much better off learning the names of the notes as soon as you can, and only using these devices if you get really stuck. If you are putting in enough practice into each step and following the instructions carefully, we hope you will never have to use these and will know the names of the notes instinctively.

Exercise

Once again, this exercise is a drill to make sure that you know all the notes covered so far.
Try to keep the rhythm of the notes you play as consistent as you can all the way through.
Playing along with a metronome is recommended, but be sure to set it at an easy, slow tempo.

Getting it right is much more important than playing it fast!

JustinGUITAR

STRING 1

STRING 2

STRING 3

STRING 4

STRING 5

STRING 6

ACCIDENTALS

MORE RHYTHMS

SCALE STUDIES

REPERTOIRE

EXERCISE 05 *Notes on strings 1 and 2*

STRING 1
STRING 2
STRING 3
STRING 4
STRING 5
STRING 6
ACCIDENTALS
MORE RHYTHMS
SCALE STUDIES
REPERTOIRE

STEP 06

Notes on strings 1 and 2 with rhythms

Next up we will be adding some simple rhythms to the notes we covered in the last exercise (the six notes on the thinnest two strings). We'll be throwing in three different note values.

If you find the rhythm even slightly tricky, then separate it out and work on tapping the rhythm before you go back to the guitar.

All the exercises are best done with a metronome, but keep it at a comfortable tempo. Save pushing your speed for later. We're building your foundations first. We want them to be solid and for you to feel confident with them!

EXERCISE 06 Notes on strings 1 and 2 with rhythms

STRING 1
STRING 2
STRING 3
STRING 4
STRING 5
STRING 6
ACCIDENTALS
MORE RHYTHMS
SCALE STUDIES
REPERTOIRE

STRING 1
STRING 2
STRING 3
STRING 4
STRING 5
STRING 6
ACCIDENTALS
MORE RHYTHMS
SCALE STUDIES
REPERTOIRE

STEP 07 | # Notes on strings 1 and 2 with rhythms and rests

In the following exercise you will get a little more practice working on your understanding of rhythm and rests.

When learning this exercise make sure to count out loud as you play. There are long gaps between notes that can make it very easy to get lost. Counting will save you from that!

You will find that as you play and read more you will start to 'feel' where you are in a bar. This will develop faster if you count and as you gain confidence in your timekeeping.

If you really need to, you can write the rhythm count under the notes, but do it in pencil and press lightly so you can rub it out later! It's much better to repeat these early exercises a few times, getting reading the notes and rhythms internalised, rather than relying on scribbling on the music you are reading. At this early stage it shouldn't be too hard—if you can't do it without using a pencil then you're not practising enough!

STRING 1

STRING 2

STRING 3

STRING 4

STRING 5

STRING 6

ACCIDENTALS

MORE RHYTHMS

SCALE STUDIES

REPERTOIRE

EXERCISE 07

Notes on strings 1 and 2 with rhythms and rests

STRING 1

STRING 2

STRING 3

STRING 4

STRING 5

STRING 6

ACCIDENTALS

MORE RHYTHMS

SCALE STUDIES

REPERTOIRE

STEP 08 Double-stops on strings 1 and 2

There is one more skill we would like to introduce to you before we learn any more notes and that is the double-stop. When we play a double-stop we essentially play two notes at the same time.

Often people, including ourselves, have found learning this a real struggle. The reason is that most teaching material regarding guitar reading focuses on reading single lines without working on double-stops or chords. We are going to save you from the same fate by introducing it early on!

What you are after here, ideally, is to learn to recognise the 'shapes' of the double-stops and how to play each group of notes. You should be thinking about it like this instead of trying to figure out each note one at a time but playing them together.

It is likely it will feel pretty tricky at first. However, you shouldn't find it takes too much practice before you start to recognise them.

On the next page you'll find that the double-stops are presented firstly by the individual notes and then by the actual double-stop where the notes are played simultaneously. Every time you find a new double-stop, you'll see the suggested fingerings written in small numbers. We highly recommend that you follow these fingerings because we are confident that they will help you position your hand in the most efficient way. At the same time by doing this we don't want to discourage anybody from exploring different fingerings.

The double stop will show the fingering only the first time it appears. This should help with the memorization of the fingerings.

Take your time with this exercise. Work your way through it and figure out the double-stop shapes. Don't try and read it straight away unless you're finding everything really easy so far. Work it out slowly and start playing with an even tempo. Only when you feel confident will you get the notes right.

EXERCISE 08 *Double-stops on strings 1 and 2*

STRING 1

STRING 2

STRING 3

STRING 4

STRING 5

STRING 6

ACCIDENTALS

MORE RHYTHMS

SCALE STUDIES

REPERTOIRE

STRING 1

STRING 2

STRING 3

STRING 4

STRING 5

STRING 6

ACCIDENTALS

MORE RHYTHMS

SCALE STUDIES

REPERTOIRE

STEP 09 # Notes on string 3 (G string)

There are only two new notes on the G string. You should find the notes in this exercise fairly easy. Just make sure you keep your eye on the rhythm!

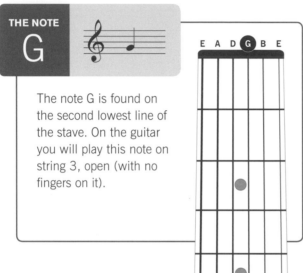

THE NOTE G

The note G is found on the second lowest line of the stave. On the guitar you will play this note on string 3, open (with no fingers on it).

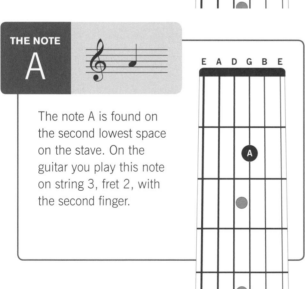

THE NOTE A

The note A is found on the second lowest space on the stave. On the guitar you play this note on string 3, fret 2, with the second finger.

Exercise

Up until now, when learning new notes, we have always kept the rhythm simple to begin with. However, as there are only two notes on the G string, we will introduce more complex rhythms straight away. To make up for it, we'll do extra practice on the notes in the following exercise when we combine these notes with the ones we have learned in previous lessons!

JustinGUITAR

STRING 1

STRING 2

STRING 3

STRING 4

STRING 5

STRING 6

ACCIDENTALS

MORE
RHYTHMS

SCALE
STUDIES

REPERTOIRE

EXERCISE
09 *Notes on string 3 (G string)*

5

10

16

21

26

31

36

STRING 1
STRING 2
STRING 3
STRING 4
STRING 5
STRING 6
ACCIDENTALS
MORE RHYTHMS
SCALE STUDIES
REPERTOIRE

STEP 10 — Notes on strings 1, 2 and 3

We've now got eight notes to read! We're covering a whole octave (from G to G) using notes with no sharps or flats (we'll be looking sharps and flats later in the course).

So now, for the first time, you can play the note G in two different places. However, take note that they are in different octaves—they're not interchangeable. Play them one after the other and you will hear that the G on string 1 is higher than the G on string 3. It is one octave higher.

Start by playing through the exercise slowly and carefully, making sure that you don't make any mistakes. Once you are confident, play the exercise with a metronome. Work very slowly, starting at around 60 bpm if you can. Only start to increase the speed when you can play it four times through without any mistakes.

If you find that you are 'learning' the notes rather than reading them, try reading the whole thing backwards. It's a great way to practise and will stop you from relying on your memory, making sure you read each note.

Another trick you might like to try is skipping staves. Try reading the 1st line, then the 3rd line, then come back to the 2nd line, then the 4th line etc. just to keep it interesting!

Also, remember that you can practise reading the notes anywhere. You could be on a train or plane, or while your partner is watching television. You don't need your guitar. Just read the music and say the note names in your head. A more advanced version of this is to imagine yourself playing the notes in your 'mind's eye'—this kind of practice can be very productive!

STRING 1

STRING 2

STRING 3

STRING 4

STRING 5

STRING 6

ACCIDENTALS

MORE RHYTHMS

SCALE STUDIES

REPERTOIRE

EXERCISE 10 — *Notes on strings 1, 2 and 3*

6

11

16

21

26

31

36

STRING 1

STRING 2

STRING 3

STRING 4

STRING 5

STRING 6

ACCIDENTALS

MORE
RHYTHMS

SCALE
STUDIES

REPERTOIRE

STEP
11 | # Notes on strings 1, 2 and 3 with rhythms

Now we are introducing rhythms to all the notes we have looked at so far!

Remember that if you are struggling you can, and should, look at the rhythm first. Just tap it out with your finger a few times through and make sure you are confident with it before trying to add the notes in.

We're still keeping the rhythms relatively simple at this point because ideally you will want to read them automatically without thinking at all. This will only come with practice and repetition.

STRING 1
STRING 2
STRING 3
STRING 4
STRING 5
STRING 6
ACCIDENTALS
MORE RHYTHMS
SCALE STUDIES
REPERTOIRE

EXERCISE 11 — Notes on strings 1, 2 and 3 with rhythms

STRING 1
STRING 2
STRING 3
STRING 4
STRING 5
STRING 6
ACCIDENTALS
MORE RHYTHMS
SCALE STUDIES
REPERTOIRE

STEP 12 — Notes on strings 1, 2 and 3 with rhythms and rests

Things get a bit more fun again now as we add in the rests as well as the rhythms.

It's very important that you play these exercises slowly and get them right.

Don't be afraid to count along as you play. You don't want to be doing this forever, but at this stage it's not a problem if it helps you get it right.

As usual, once you can play through the exercise, use your metronome, starting very slowly and building up speed only when you can play it all the way through with 100% accuracy.

Also, don't forget to keep a good overall technique while reading. This means:

- with your fretting-hand, press only as hard as is needed to produce a clear sound
- with your picking-hand, pick in the middle of your dynamic range (not too quiet and not too loud)
- make sure that both your arms, shoulders and neck are completely relaxed
- keep breathing!

STEP 13 — Strings 1, 2 and 3 with double-stops

Now we're really working it!

We're going to be reading two notes at a time (double-stops) along with all eight notes AND rhythms! This should hopefully be challenging (not disheartening) and help to improve your reading skills.

Before attempting to read it, take a minute to look at all the double-stops and work out how they are played. Try to learn the shapes of the intervals and how they're played on the guitar neck—this will take practice and repetition. There is no shortcut.

Once you know how to play all the double-stops, start to play slowly through the whole exercise. Again, when you are feeling up to it, get the metronome on!

Hybrid Picking

You'll notice that some of the double-stops are on not-adjacent strings (e.g. G string and high E string). When we're playing finger-style this doesn't present a big challenge because it's easy to skip a string but what happens when we're using a pick? There's a variety of ways to do this but for the time being we suggest simply using hybrid picking. Hybrid picking is a picking style which combines using a pick and one or more fingers in the picking-hand.

The easiest way to approach this is by picking the lowest note with the pick while picking the highest note with a finger. Normally the most common finger used is the middle finger simply because the pick is held between thumb and index and the middle is the 'next one up'. Anyhow, feel free to explore using the ring or little finger as well.

EXERCISE 12 *Notes on strings 1, 2 and 3 with rhythms and rests*

STRING 1

STRING 2

STRING 3

STRING 4

STRING 5

STRING 6

ACCIDENTALS

MORE RHYTHMS

SCALE STUDIES

REPERTOIRE

STRING 1

STRING 2

STRING 3

STRING 4

STRING 5

STRING 6

ACCIDENTALS

MORE RHYTHMS

SCALE STUDIES

REPERTOIRE

EXERCISE 13 *Strings 1, 2 and 3 with double-stops*

6

11

16

21

26

31

36

JustinGUITAR

STRING 1
STRING 2
STRING 3
STRING 4
STRING 5
STRING 6
ACCIDENTALS
MORE RHYTHMS
SCALE STUDIES
REPERTOIRE

STEP 14

Your first duet

Ready to play with someone else? Reading duet pieces is a great way to test your reading skills and is a lot of fun.

You could do this with a friend or your teacher, or even someone on another instrument who can read music.

In these examples, player one should always read the top stave of each pair and player two should always read the bottom stave.

Start by deciding on a part to learn and be sure both players can play it confidently before attempting to play it as a duet, otherwise it's likely you'll end up in chaos, which is not too enjoyable!

One person will lead (usually player one) and will count in one bar with '1, 2, 3, 4'. This is in itself something that is worth practicing. Often students don't count in time simply because they never do it and they don't have a system to count. After the count-in they either slow down or speed up once the piece has started. When you count in a piece, start by 'reading' the first couple of bars in your head to get the right speed. Essentially you need to hear in your head how fast a quarter-note beat is. If you can hear that then you are ready to count in. Then both players start on the first beat of the first bar of the piece.

It's a good idea to play along with a metronome. If you don't have one available, be sure that at least one player is tapping their foot to help keep the rhythm. Alternatively, if both of you are tapping your feet, make sure you are in time with each other.

Eventually we would recommend that both players learn both parts. After playing through the whole exercise you can immediately swap parts and play it again.

STRING 1

STRING 2

STRING 3

STRING 4

STRING 5

STRING 6

ACCIDENTALS

MORE RHYTHMS

SCALE STUDIES

REPERTOIRE

EXERCISE

14 *Duet #1*

STRING 1

STRING 2

STRING 3

STRING 4

STRING 5

STRING 6

ACCIDENTALS

MORE RHYTHMS

SCALE STUDIES

REPERTOIRE

STRING 1

STRING 2

STRING 3

STRING 4

STRING 5

STRING 6

ACCIDENTALS

MORE RHYTHMS

SCALE STUDIES

REPERTOIRE

STEP 15 Introducing $\frac{3}{4}$ time

In this lesson we're going to introduce a new time signature. That means we're going to change the number of beats in a bar!

Everything we've seen so far has been in $\frac{4}{4}$ time, which has four beats in each bar. Now we're going to look at $\frac{3}{4}$ time, which has three beats in each bar.

It's no different to playing in $\frac{4}{4}$, other than you'll find less notes in the bar. It also has a different mood—many people feel it straight away as a Waltz.

We're starting out nice and simple, with notes on only the thinnest three strings as well as easy rhythms.

A great way to start is to ignore the notes and just tap out the rhythm with your finger on a table. Make sure you are comfortable reading the rhythm before you add in the notes and you'll find it a lot easier!

So, have some fun with this new adventure! Just remember to keep it slow. Don't be afraid to count along as you read when you are starting out. However, try to make the feel of the rhythm instinctive eventually.

This study uses quarter-note and whole note rests. Please be aware that in $\frac{3}{4}$ time, a whole note rest is worth 3 beats (the length of the bar).

STRING 1

STRING 2

STRING 3

STRING 4

STRING 5

STRING 6

ACCIDENTALS

MORE RHYTHMS

SCALE STUDIES

REPERTOIRE

EXERCISE 15 *Introducing* $\frac{3}{4}$ *time*

STRING 1
STRING 2
STRING 3
STRING 4
STRING 5
STRING 6
ACCIDENTALS
MORE RHYTHMS
SCALE STUDIES
REPERTOIRE

STEP 16 $\frac{3}{4}$ Study

Now you're more familiar with $\frac{3}{4}$ time we're going to do another study which introduces some double-stops.

Remember that the aim with double-stops is to try and recognise the 'blocks' and know how to finger each group of notes. You shouldn't always have to calculate each note separately.

Have fun!

JustinGUITAR

STRING 1

STRING 2

STRING 3

STRING 4

STRING 5

STRING 6

ACCIDENTALS

MORE RHYTHMS

SCALE STUDIES

REPERTOIRE

EXERCISE 16 ¾ *Study*

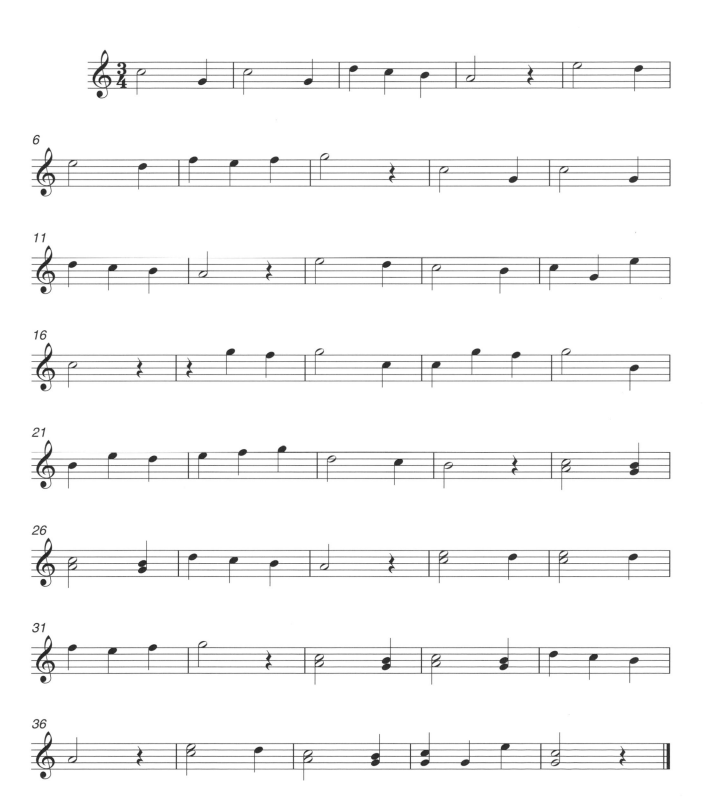

STRING 1

STRING 2

STRING 3

STRING 4

STRING 5

STRING 6

ACCIDENTALS

MORE RHYTHMS

SCALE STUDIES

REPERTOIRE

STEP 17 Notes on string 4 (D string)

There are three new notes on D string.

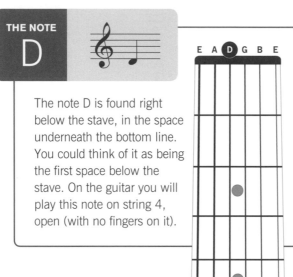

THE NOTE D

The note D is found right below the stave, in the space underneath the bottom line. You could think of it as being the first space below the stave. On the guitar you will play this note on string 4, open (with no fingers on it).

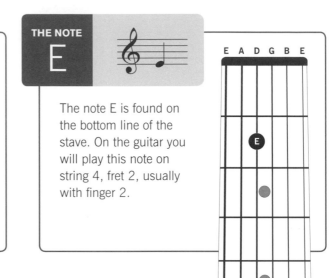

THE NOTE E

The note E is found on the bottom line of the stave. On the guitar you will play this note on string 4, fret 2, usually with finger 2.

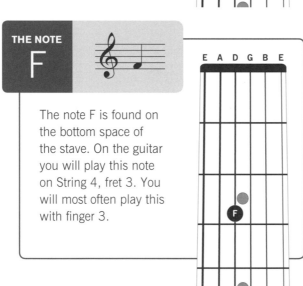

THE NOTE F

The note F is found on the bottom space of the stave. On the guitar you will play this note on String 4, fret 3. You will most often play this with finger 3.

Exercise

This exercise keeps the rhythm simple so you can focus on the notes—remember that you can work on reading even if you don't have your guitar with you by saying the notes out loud! If you find it tricky remembering the notes, try reading backwards or skipping every alternate line. Anything to keep you from just focusing on the patterns of the notes: in the end you'll have to be able to read them from sight.

STRING 1

STRING 2

STRING 3

STRING 4

STRING 5

STRING 6

ACCIDENTALS

MORE RHYTHMS

SCALE STUDIES

REPERTOIRE

EXERCISE 17

Notes on string 4 (D string)

6

11

16

21

26

31

36

STRING 1
STRING 2
STRING 3
STRING 4
STRING 5
STRING 6
ACCIDENTALS
MORE RHYTHMS
SCALE STUDIES
REPERTOIRE

STEP

18 | Notes on the thinnest four strings

In this exercise we're looking at all the notes from the thinnest 4 strings, no rhythm variations so you can focus on the notes.

At this stage you need to be well aware of the note names as well as the octave of the note—which E is written? String 1 open or string 4, fret 2? It's very important that you play the notes in the right octave.

Make sure you stick to consistent fingering using fingers 1, 2 and 3 in frets 1, 2, 3. Sometimes you might need to deviate from this (for example, when you play double-stops or chords) but it's a very good idea to have this as a 'default setting'. Try to keep the fingers hovering over the corresponding fret (e.g. finger 1 hovers over fret 1; finger 2 hovers over fret 2, etc.). This will keep your hand consistently stretched and it might feel slightly uncomfortable at first but as with most things, with some practice it will feel natural.

The key to this is to position the fretting-hand thumb in the lower part of the guitar neck (closer to the floor) without bending the wrist too much. The whole hand position (hand, wrist, forearm and arm) needs to be very relaxed so try to relax more and more as you play. Relaxing is something that gets easier with practicing!

JustinGUITAR

STRING 1
STRING 2
STRING 3
STRING 4
STRING 5
STRING 6
ACCIDENTALS
MORE RHYTHMS
SCALE STUDIES
REPERTOIRE

EXERCISE 18 *Notes on the thinnest four strings*

STRING 1

STRING 2

STRING 3

STRING 4

STRING 5

STRING 6

ACCIDENTALS

MORE
RHYTHMS

SCALE
STUDIES

REPERTOIRE

STEP 19 | Notes on the thinnest four strings with rhythms

In this exercise we're going to be looking at all the notes from the thinnest 4 strings, but this time adding in some rhythms.

Remember to tap out the rhythms without the notes if you are struggling with the rhythm, and say the note out loud without the rhythm if you are struggling with the notes. You can do this without a guitar too, on your way to work/school, in bed before sleeping or well…on the toilet!

STRING 1
STRING 2
STRING 3
STRING 4
STRING 5
STRING 6
ACCIDENTALS
MORE RHYTHMS
SCALE STUDIES
REPERTOIRE

EXERCISE 19 *Notes on the thinnest four strings with rhythms*

STRING 1
STRING 2
STRING 3
STRING 4
STRING 5
STRING 6
ACCIDENTALS
MORE RHYTHMS
SCALE STUDIES
REPERTOIRE

STEP 20 — Notes on the thinnest four strings with rhythms and rests

Now we're getting a bit more real as we'll be looking at all the notes from the thinnest four strings, along with rhythms and rests.

When you have a lot of rests it can be very helpful to count along. We recommend tapping your foot along whenever you play but learning to count the rhythm out loud can be very helpful too.

One way to do this is to count the rhythms and say the notes out loud, and *whisper* the rests. This way you hear the rhythms as you speak them. A lot of people find using this technique a big help when learning to read rhythms. For some, this may seem a little easy, but it's good practice for when things get a little more challenging and you have more complex rhythms to deal with!

1   2   (3)   4   1   2   3   (4)   1   2   (3)   4   1   (2)   3   4

The breakdown

It can be very helpful to understand the breakdown of skills you are using now. It will really help you find and remedy any consistent mistakes you are making. You can break this down into two main areas, reading and technique.

Reading can be further broken down into four parts: note recognition, knowledge of notes on the fretboard, rhythmic comprehension (including counting) and finally the 'flow'—how easily you can play what you read.

Technique breaks down into more physical elements: picking-hand, fretting-hand, relaxation and tapping your foot.

If you are having problems at this stage, can you identify which element is causing you problems? How can you refine the exercises to specifically work on this problem? Have a think and make a note!

JustinGUITAR

STRING 1

STRING 2

STRING 3

STRING 4

STRING 5

STRING 6

ACCIDENTALS

MORE RHYTHMS

SCALE STUDIES

REPERTOIRE

EXERCISE 20

Notes on the thinnest four strings with rhythms and rests

STRING 1
STRING 2
STRING 3
STRING 4
STRING 5
STRING 6
ACCIDENTALS
MORE RHYTHMS
SCALE STUDIES
REPERTOIRE

STEP 21 | Thinnest four strings with double-stops

Now we'll introduce double-stops with what we've learned so far. As we have more notes available, some of the notes are a lot further apart than we've had before.

You will almost certainly have to start out by reading the notes one at a time and working out the fingering, but in the long term you are aiming to recognise the note pairs and know instinctively how to play them.

Some note pairs, like octaves and pairs of open strings, are very common and you'll find it a big help to learn to recognise them right away. Like everything else, it's down to putting in the practice time. The more you read the more you will become familiar with the common pairs and, eventually, small chords!

JustinGUITAR

STRING 1

STRING 2

STRING 3

STRING 4

STRING 5

STRING 6

ACCIDENTALS

MORE
RHYTHMS

SCALE
STUDIES

REPERTOIRE

EXERCISE
21 *Thinnest four strings with double-stops*

STRING 1

STRING 2

STRING 3

STRING 4

STRING 5

STRING 6

ACCIDENTALS

MORE RHYTHMS

SCALE STUDIES

REPERTOIRE

STEP 22 — Thinnest four strings with small chords

When learning to read, chords can look very scary. We've found that the best way to tackle them is to introduce them early on so people can get used to them.

What you will find is that because of the layout of the guitar there are a limited number of possibilities. Common chords will become easier to recognise than you might think. However, again it's going to take some practice.

We've firstly written the notes that make up the chord and then made variations later in the exercise so you can explore a little, hopefully without feeling too overwhelmed.

If you're playing with a pick, then simply strum the chords. Try to avoid a slow strum (one where you can hear the individual strings). Strumming a chord should sound like one big sound and not four sounds very close together!

Take it slow and use your experience with double-stops to help you recognise the 'blocks'. Just as children learn to read words by spelling the letters out slowly, you are likely to be reading chords in a similar way to start off with. Don't feel discouraged if it feels difficult. Practice is the solution!

What is difficult is when you encounter music written by someone who doesn't understand the tuning and layout of the notes on the guitar and writes impossible things! Piano players that write arrangements are often guilty of this because they have access to more notes than us, particularly notes that are close together which are physically easy on piano but very difficult on the guitar. If you ever encounter this kind of problem just get as many notes as you can on the first read and edit the music later to make the part playable.

Be nice!

As a side note, if you encounter a chord in a notated part that can't be played on the guitar, it's better to edit the music yourself than point out the error to the arranger, particularly in a rehearsal situation. It's better to do what you can without making a big deal of it. It's quite common to meet producers or musical directors who are not too happy about players that 'make a noise'. It's generally better to be nice than clever!

JustinGUITAR

STRING 1

STRING 2

STRING 3

STRING 4

STRING 5

STRING 6

ACCIDENTALS

MORE RHYTHMS

SCALE STUDIES

REPERTOIRE

EXERCISE 22

Thinnest four strings with small chords

let ring throughout

STRING 1

STRING 2

STRING 3

STRING 4

STRING 5

STRING 6

ACCIDENTALS

MORE RHYTHMS

SCALE STUDIES

REPERTOIRE

STEP 23 — Introducing eighth-notes

So far we have only been looking at very basic rhythms that fell on a beat and now we will look at what happens between the beats.

If a note falls halfway between the beats we count it as an 'and', usually written as a '+' if the count is written out.

A note worth one beat is called a 'quarter-note' (crotchet). If we cut a quarter in half we end up with two eighth-notes (also called 'quavers'). Hopefully you remember that two eighths make one quarter!

If you have not done this type of counting before, make sure you count it out loud and get used to vocalising it!

'1   and   2   and   3   and   4   and'

It's important to create a habit of counting. Most of the rhythmic problems of reading are because we stop counting.

When you're reading something with eighth-notes you need to count '1 and 2 and 3 and 4 and' all the time, not just when the eighth-note appears. If you only start counting eighth-notes when you see one you won't be prepared and the note will most likely be out of time. If you see even one eighth-note, just start counting the 'and' from the beginning.

So start by counting out loud and tap your foot on the beat (just the numbers). That's important—make sure that your foot taps ON THE BEAT and not every time you play a note!

Playing all the examples in this book with a metronome is very helpful. Make sure that your foot is tapping with the metronome.

Picking direction

This is also a good time to introduce you to picking-hand directions which apply only to playing with the pick. The idea is that we use our picking-hand to help us 'count' our way through the bar. Start by counting '1 and 2 and 3 and 4 and' out loud and at the same time play a down-stroke (towards the floor) on each 'number' and an up-stroke (towards the ceiling) for each 'and'. So you should have '1' (down), 'and' (up), '2' (down), etc. It's important to FEEL the connection between counting and moving the hand. Doing the two simultaneously without feeling their connection won't cut it. Slow it right down until you feel the connection between the counting and the hand movement. We want to ingrain this system so that we associate down-strokes with any note on the beat and up-strokes with any note on the 'and'.

The eighth-notes ('quavers') can appear in a few different ways on the page: an eighth-note can be shown as a single note or if there are multiple eighth-notes, they might be grouped together—the exact grouping depends on the time signature. The 'grouping' of notes is called 'beaming', as stems of the notes are joined together by a horizontal 'beam'.

In $\frac{4}{4}$, eighth-notes are normally found individually, or in beams of 2 and 4. In the first line of the exercise you'll find the different layout of eighth-notes.

In the last bar of the first line you'll also find a new type of note-head which is called 'slash' rhythmic notation. This doesn't refer to any particular pitch and it's normally used in combination with chord names to describe the rhythm that needs to be played.

JustinGUITAR

STRING 1

STRING 2

STRING 3

STRING 4

STRING 5

STRING 6

ACCIDENTALS

MORE RHYTHMS

SCALE STUDIES

REPERTOIRE

EXERCISE 23 *Introducing eighth-notes*

STRING 1

STRING 2

STRING 3

STRING 4

STRING 5

STRING 6

ACCIDENTALS

MORE RHYTHMS

SCALE STUDIES

REPERTOIRE

STEP 24 Notes on string 5 (the A string)

So, we're getting down onto the 'ledger lines' now—the notes below the stave. Ledger lines extend below and above the stave. While at first they might seem complicated, you'll be pleasantly surprised how quickly you will recognise them and be able to play them. We have three new notes on the A string.

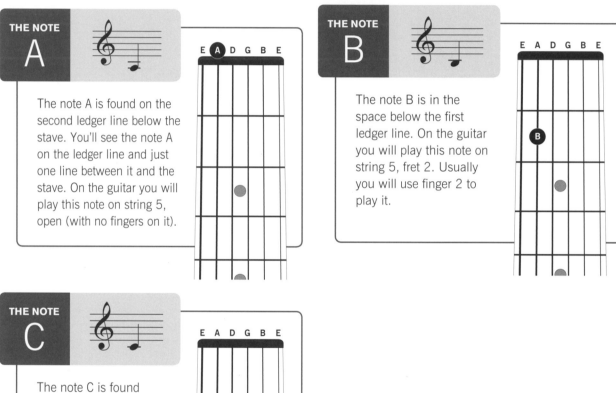

THE NOTE A

The note A is found on the second ledger line below the stave. You'll see the note A on the ledger line and just one line between it and the stave. On the guitar you will play this note on string 5, open (with no fingers on it).

THE NOTE B

The note B is in the space below the first ledger line. On the guitar you will play this note on string 5, fret 2. Usually you will use finger 2 to play it.

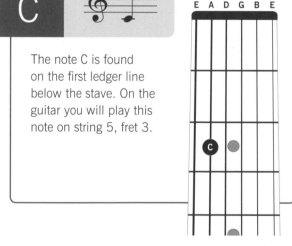

THE NOTE C

The note C is found on the first ledger line below the stave. On the guitar you will play this note on string 5, fret 3.

As usual, this first exercise is just to get you used to these new notes. Take it slow, get it right and then try reading it backwards, alternating bars or whatever you can to stop yourself from memorising it and getting plenty of practice. However, as soon as you're confident, you should start mixing it up with notes you know already.

EXERCISE 24 *Notes on string 5 (the A string)*

6

11

16

21

26

31

36

STRING 1
STRING 2
STRING 3
STRING 4
STRING 5
STRING 6
ACCIDENTALS
MORE RHYTHMS
SCALE STUDIES
REPERTOIRE

STRING 1

STRING 2

STRING 3

STRING 4

STRING 5

STRING 6

ACCIDENTALS

MORE RHYTHMS

SCALE STUDIES

REPERTOIRE

STEP 25 — Notes on the thinnest five strings

Once you are confident with the notes on string 5 (and not before) you should mix it up with all the notes you have learned previously. It's important to do it this way and it will help you learn it as fast as possible.

Most people find it tricky when they first start trying to read ledger lines, but it does start to get familiar sooner than you might think. It's typical to find them harder than 'normal' notes. However, at the end of the day it's just practice like everything else!

The open A will be one you'll probably see quite often as an open string. C will be another one that you'll just get used to: being on the first ledger line makes it pretty obvious.

Do work these in thoroughly and don't be in too much of a hurry to get that last string done. The notes on string 6 have even more ledger lines and do take some getting used to!

Good luck!

STEP 26 — Thinnest five strings with rhythms

Now that you've mastered the note reading part of the thinnest five strings we'll introduce some rhythms too.

The rhythms are still pretty basic and gaining confidence in your ability to read rhythms is very important. The more you read, the more familiar you will become with both the notes and the rhythms. In the long term you will want your recognition to become instinctive—instant recognition of the notes, rhythms and even double-stops and chords.

Nobody expects you to be developing this 'instinct' at this early stage but you should be open to allowing it and be happy when it starts to feel automatic. It's much like learning to read letters on a page—you start off by spelling them out, but after a while it flows without having to think too much.

It's all down to lots of repetition—the more you do, the easier and faster you will recognise the notes and rhythms. It will eventually become pretty automated.

You should always avoid mistakes of course! However, it's also important to learn to carry on playing even if you fluff a note or two. Try to keep your place. Imagine if you were in a band all playing together: you wouldn't want the whole band to stop if you made a mistake. It's rhythm that carries the most weight in music, so try to develop solid time and the ability to keep counting even if you miss a note or two. That way you'll always come back in at the right place! This is where reading music helps us develop one of the most useful habits ever: always looking ahead!

Justin GUITAR

STRING 1

STRING 2

STRING 3

STRING 4

STRING 5

STRING 6

ACCIDENTALS

MORE RHYTHMS

SCALE STUDIES

REPERTOIRE

EXERCISE 25

Notes on the thinnest five strings

6

11

16

21

26

31

36

STRING 1

STRING 2

STRING 3

STRING 4

STRING 5

STRING 6

ACCIDENTALS

MORE RHYTHMS

SCALE STUDIES

REPERTOIRE

EXERCISE 26

Thinnest five strings with rhythms

STRING 1

STRING 2

STRING 3

STRING 4

STRING 5

STRING 6

ACCIDENTALS

MORE RHYTHMS

SCALE STUDIES

REPERTOIRE

STEP 27 — Thinnest five strings with rhythms and rests

Rests are just as important to read as rhythms. Make sure you are as comfortable playing silence as you are the notes!

It's important to learn to 'feel' the rests. If you don't feel the rests, then they are nothing. Rests are silence, which is a 'thing'. The ability to produce silence is just as important as our ability to make noise.

When learning how to 'feel' silence it can help to do or say something in that space, perhaps thinking of a sound or a word. It can also help to move your picking-hand without hitting the strings, effectively 'playing silence'. You may find it much easier to feel the rest if you put in an action.

You might have noticed that musicians often nod their head during the silence. This is a very common way of playing and feeling silence. It's important to feel the 'pulse' of the music.

Try a few things with this exercise and see what works for you. Just don't let the rests be 'nothing'.

As usual, it comes down to familiarity. So, practise them as much as you can and 'allow' the reading process to become natural. I know it sounds a bit like hippy nonsense, but there is quite a bit of psychology involved in learning. 'Allowing' yourself to absorb the information deeply is important. Consciously and deliberately 'allowing' (not forcing) can really help. Let the notes, rhythms and rests penetrate deep into your mind so they become close and well known friends!

STEP 28 — Thinnest five strings with double-stops

We're back revisiting double-stops again and there is nothing new conceptually— just a few extra notes to deal with!

You will notice that there are certain combinations of double-stops that are common and sound really cool. Try to make a note of the ones you commonly see and like the sound of. Note down what interval they are (how far apart in pitch) and what notes often come before or after them.

You will often find double-stops in a series so try to recognise the 'double-stop phrases' as well. In open position (the position we are using for all our study in these books) you will especially find very common sets.

A good resource for practising double-stops and chords in open position is the Segovia edition of the 20 Studies by Fernando Sor. The book is very common Classical repertoire and certainly worth looking up for extra reading practice when you have finished this book!

STRING 1

STRING 2

STRING 3

STRING 4

STRING 5

STRING 6

ACCIDENTALS

MORE RHYTHMS

SCALE STUDIES

REPERTOIRE

EXERCISE 27

Thinnest five strings with rhythms and rests

STRING 1

STRING 2

STRING 3

STRING 4

STRING 5

STRING 6

ACCIDENTALS

MORE RHYTHMS

SCALE STUDIES

REPERTOIRE

EXERCISE 28 *Thinnest five strings with double-stops*

STRING 1
STRING 2
STRING 3
STRING 4
STRING 5
STRING 6
ACCIDENTALS
MORE RHYTHMS
SCALE STUDIES
REPERTOIRE

STEP 29 Thinnest five strings with chords

Big block chords are always tricky to read, especially when there are five or more notes. With a little practice you will learn to quickly recognise common chord shapes because they come up a lot, and much more often that random-note chord clusters.

Experienced readers will recognise more chords than a novice, but on big unusual five or six note chords, the vast majority of guitar players will have to slow down or stop and figure out the best way to play it.

In this book, we're staying in open position and the chord complexity is fairly simple, so most of the chords you'll find here are commonly used.

Make sure you note the 'let ring' at the start. The individual notes are there to help you find the chords!

STEP 30 Duet #2

Next up we have a lovely duet to have fun with if you have a jam buddy (i.e. a buddy you can jam with!).

If you're on your own, you can either record one part and play along with it or use a looper pedal to record one part and play the other. Home recording is definitely worth a look—it's great fun and inexpensive to get started these days. Alternatively, if you go for the looper pedal approach we'd recommend playing along with a metronome. Don't forget to give yourself a count in!

JustinGUITAR

STRING 1
STRING 2
STRING 3
STRING 4
STRING 5
STRING 6
ACCIDENTALS
MORE RHYTHMS
SCALE STUDIES
REPERTOIRE

EXERCISE 29 *Thinnest five strings with chords*

let ring throughout

STRING 1

STRING 2

STRING 3

STRING 4

STRING 5

STRING 6

ACCIDENTALS

MORE RHYTHMS

SCALE STUDIES

REPERTOIRE

EXERCISE
30   *Duet #2*

STRING 1
STRING 2
STRING 3
STRING 4
STRING 5
STRING 6
ACCIDENTALS
MORE RHYTHMS
SCALE STUDIES
REPERTOIRE

let ring whenever possible

STRING 1

STRING 2

STRING 3

STRING 4

STRING 5

STRING 6

ACCIDENTALS

MORE RHYTHMS

SCALE STUDIES

REPERTOIRE

STEP

31 | Introducing $\frac{2}{4}$

At some point you're likely to come across the time signature $\frac{2}{4}$. This time signature has two quarter-notes in a bar.

Many people wonder why $\frac{2}{4}$ songs are not simply written in $\frac{4}{4}$ time and it's because of the strong and weak beats in a bar. In $\frac{4}{4}$ time beat 1 is the strongest and beat 3 is a little weaker (we've labelled it on the diagram below, 'quite strong'). Beats 2 and 4 are equally the weakest beats.

So in $\frac{2}{4}$ we only have strong beats, and we no longer have that 'slightly weaker' beat 3, which changes the feel of the music. It is common to find this confusing when you first encounter it but like many musical things, playing it will help you to understand it.

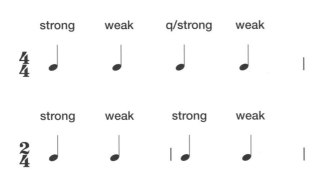

JustinGUITAR

STRING 1
STRING 2
STRING 3
STRING 4
STRING 5
STRING 6
ACCIDENTALS
MORE RHYTHMS
SCALE STUDIES
REPERTOIRE

EXERCISE 31 *Introducing* 2/4

STRING 1
STRING 2
STRING 3
STRING 4
STRING 5
STRING 6
ACCIDENTALS
MORE RHYTHMS
SCALE STUDIES
REPERTOIRE

STEP 32 Notes on the thickest E string

We're nearly there—this is the last set of new notes for this book! These last three lines use quite a few ledger lines. Most people find them a bit tricky. We sure did when we started! However, as we've said before, it will become familiar sooner than you'd expect. Hopefully you've gone through that experience with string 5. These are no different—just a few extra ledger lines!

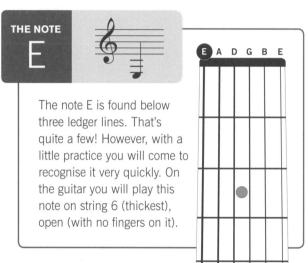

THE NOTE E

The note E is found below three ledger lines. That's quite a few! However, with a little practice you will come to recognise it very quickly. On the guitar you will play this note on string 6 (thickest), open (with no fingers on it).

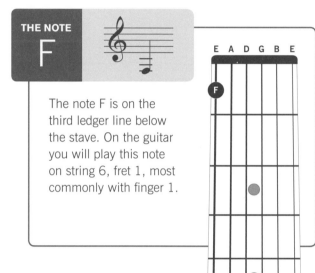

THE NOTE F

The note F is on the third ledger line below the stave. On the guitar you will play this note on string 6, fret 1, most commonly with finger 1.

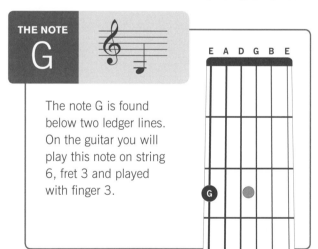

THE NOTE G

The note G is found below two ledger lines. On the guitar you will play this note on string 6, fret 3 and played with finger 3.

Congratulations!

You now know ALL the notes in the open position, which is a massive achievement. Well done on making it this far! From now on you are consolidating this information and becoming more fluent in reading notation.

As usual, this first exercise is just focused on these new notes and then we'll be working them in!

EXERCISE 32 — Notes on the thickest E string

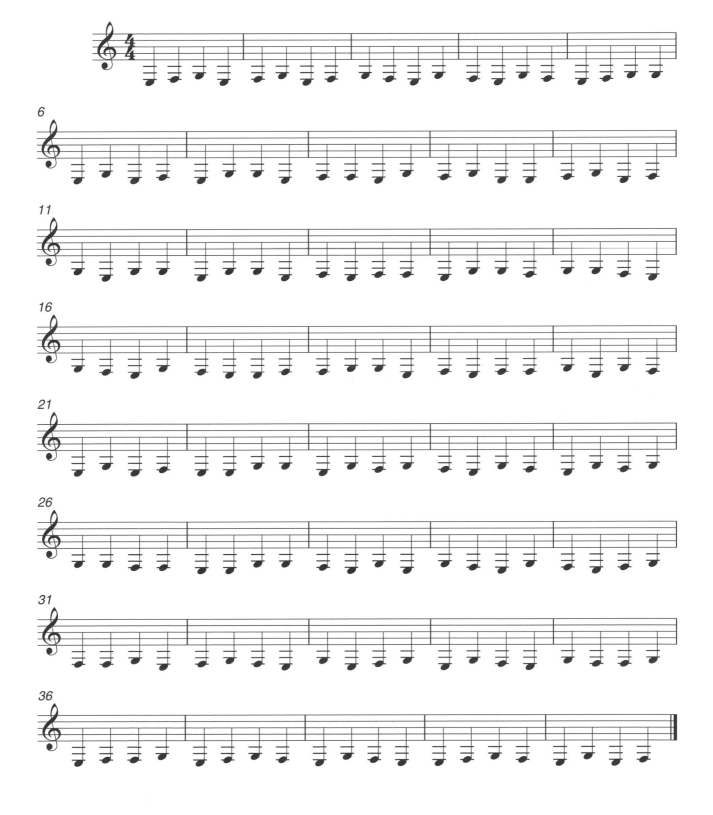

STRING 1
STRING 2
STRING 3
STRING 4
STRING 5
STRING 6
ACCIDENTALS
MORE RHYTHMS
SCALE STUDIES
REPERTOIRE

STRING 1

STRING 2

STRING 3

STRING 4

STRING 5

STRING 6

ACCIDENTALS

MORE RHYTHMS

SCALE STUDIES

REPERTOIRE

STEP
33 | Ledger lines

Most people find reading the ledger lines a little tricky, so welcome to a seriously nasty page!

In the following exercise we'll be looking at all the notes that have ledger lines below the stave. From C down to E, work it through a few times and try to get as familiar as you can with these dots.

You might find sometimes they get a bit 'blurred' but remember that you can also look at them as being 'relative' to the notes around them—look at the interval jumps between the notes.

Remember—the solution is practice!

Do this a lot and you'll have it down in no time. Skip over it because it's hard and it will always be hard!

You will definitely reap the benefits of these harder exercises so don't shy away. Facing and overcoming difficulties makes better people as well as better musicians.

Smooth seas don't make great sailors.

STRING 1
STRING 2
STRING 3
STRING 4
STRING 5
STRING 6
ACCIDENTALS
MORE RHYTHMS
SCALE STUDIES
REPERTOIRE

EXERCISE 33 *Ledger lines*

STRING 1

STRING 2

STRING 3

STRING 4

STRING 5

STRING 6

ACCIDENTALS

MORE RHYTHMS

SCALE STUDIES

REPERTOIRE

STEP 34 — Notes on all six strings!

We're there—now we're going to be reading all the notes on all six strings. Well done you!

You've come far and we hope the journey has been smooth and fun. This last set of notes to learn is no more painful than the last. And it's going to be easier than the ledger line hell you had in the last lesson!

I hope that you will not need to refer back to previous lessons to remember the notes—it's VERY important that you have every note position on the stave and every note on the neck memorised. If you have any that you find yourself getting consistently getting stuck on, make a special note to work on those ones and work them in as soon as you can. Perhaps go back and revise the exercises that focus on those notes or rhythms.

You MUST know the notes from memory. They're no good to you anywhere else!

STEP 35 — All six strings with rhythms

We're sure you know the drill by now. We have the notes, now we're introducing rhythms to them.

There's nothing new or more complicated here. Just take your time, keep it slow and you'll be fluent before you know it.

STEP 36 — All six strings with rhythms and rests

The drill continues. We're now adding in rests!

Just a gentle reminder. Rests mean silence, so make sure you have all your strings muted.

JustinGUITAR

STRING 1

STRING 2

STRING 3

STRING 4

STRING 5

STRING 6

ACCIDENTALS

MORE RHYTHMS

SCALE STUDIES

REPERTOIRE

EXERCISE 34 *Notes on all six strings!*

STRING 1

STRING 2

STRING 3

STRING 4

STRING 5

STRING 6

ACCIDENTALS

MORE RHYTHMS

SCALE STUDIES

REPERTOIRE

EXERCISE 35 *All six strings with rhythms*

STRING 1
STRING 2
STRING 3
STRING 4
STRING 5
STRING 6
ACCIDENTALS
MORE RHYTHMS
SCALE STUDIES
REPERTOIRE

EXERCISE 36 *All six strings with rhythms and rests*

STRING 1

STRING 2

STRING 3

STRING 4

STRING 5

STRING 6

ACCIDENTALS

MORE
RHYTHMS

SCALE
STUDIES

REPERTOIRE

STEP 37 | All six strings with double-stops

It's getting a bit tricky now, so don't be alarmed if you find this pretty hard. It is.

Reading double-stops and chords is more than twice as hard. There are two or more notes to read AND you have to figure out how to play them at once!

Take it slow and easy. At these early stages don't be afraid of stopping and working everything out. You need to figure many things out: how you will play the common shapes? What fingering is easiest? Is there more than one fingering?

Any of you with reading experience or good knowledge will know that almost every note can be played in more than one place on the fretboard. Some double-stops have an alternative fingering, some of which may be easier. However, for these studies we would recommend that you stick with open position and get to know it as well as you can. Explore other positions (parts of the neck) only when you are confident in open position.

EXERCISE 37 — All six strings with double-stops

STRING 1
STRING 2
STRING 3
STRING 4
STRING 5
STRING 6
ACCIDENTALS
MORE RHYTHMS
SCALE STUDIES
REPERTOIRE

STRING 1
STRING 2
STRING 3
STRING 4
STRING 5
STRING 6
ACCIDENTALS
MORE RHYTHMS
SCALE STUDIES
REPERTOIRE

STEP 38 — All six strings with chords

There's a lot going on now that we have chords on all 6 strings now! The chords in this exercise are all commonly played so try to remember their visual form.

You might find it easier to see big chords in smaller groups that are recognisable as 'blocks'. You could think of it like combining the words 'type' and 'writer' together to make 'typewriter'—combining two blocks to make the full chord. We call this process 'chunking' and the brain does it all the time.

Smaller blocks are easier to digest quickly and can also help to figure out the required fingering quickly. This is especially important in later stages when you might be looking for chord grips all over the neck.

At this stage we are only using natural notes, so the key of C. It's a good idea to start trying to recognise the shapes of the 'blocks' of notes: the intervallic spacing between the notes. This is all before we add in the complications of sharps and flats of course!

Justin GUITAR

STRING 1
STRING 2
STRING 3
STRING 4
STRING 5
STRING 6
ACCIDENTALS
MORE RHYTHMS
SCALE STUDIES
REPERTOIRE

EXERCISE 38 *All six strings with chords*

STRING 1

STRING 2

STRING 3

STRING 4

STRING 5

STRING 6

ACCIDENTALS

MORE RHYTHMS

SCALE STUDIES

REPERTOIRE

STEP 39 Random note study #1

So, now we're into our first random note study. This kind of exercise is a whole new challenge because, if you've realised it or not, you will have been recognising interval movements between notes. When that's taken away and the jumps are a lot bigger, you need to focus more on what the note is and where it's played.

We recommend going through the exercise a few times, naming the notes out loud without playing the notes before you start trying to play it. It's great for your note recognition and will help you recognise any weaknesses. Perhaps you need more work on ledger lines or maybe you need to work on naming the notes quicker.

If you have a jam buddy, you can ask them to name random notes. Then, you must find them on the neck as fast as you can. Of course there is more than one way to play each note, so try to find them in the area that is giving you the most trouble, not where you find it easiest!

EXERCISE 39 — Random note study #1

STRING 1

STRING 2

STRING 3

STRING 4

STRING 5

STRING 6

ACCIDENTALS

MORE RHYTHMS

SCALE STUDIES

REPERTOIRE

STRING 1

STRING 2

STRING 3

STRING 4

STRING 5

STRING 6

ACCIDENTALS

MORE RHYTHMS

SCALE STUDIES

REPERTOIRE

STEP 40 | # Accidentals

See that can of worms? Yep, that really big one. Well, we're going to tip it all over everything you learned so far!

In this lesson we're introducing a really important part of reading music, sharps and flats.

A **sharp** (♯) raises the pitch of the following note by one semitone (1 fret). You can remember this by thinking that if you sit on something sharp you would jump UP.

A **flat** (♭) lowers the pitch of the following note by one semitone (one fret). You can remember this by imagining the height of a car getting lower with a flat tyre.

A **natural** (♮) means that you will play a natural note (not a sharp of flat).

Before we put this into practice, let's first dispel the confusion surrounding the word 'accidental'. Trust us—they're no accident.

Very soon we will be looking at playing in different keys. If you know any music theory, you might already know that in all keys except C major/A minor, some notes are consistently sharpened or flattened. For example, in the key of A major, all F, G and C notes are played as F♯, G♯ and C♯ respectively. This should be represented in the key signature, displayed at the beginning of each line of music.

Key signature for A major

Accidentals are sharps or flats that are NOT present in the key signature. They last for the remainder of the bar they are placed in, so if you see a ♯ before an F, all other Fs in the same octave in that bar will be played as F♯ for the remainder of the bar. An F in the next bar will be played as a natural but can sometimes have a natural in brackets before it to remind you— these are called 'courtesy accidentals'.

This first exercise uses only the notes we've looked at on the thin E String: E, F and G.

Let's start looking at G, which was fret 3. G♯ is on fret 4, G♭ is on fret 2. We hope that is clear for you.

Now let's look at F which is found on fret 1. F♯ will be one higher than the natural note, so it will be on fret 2—the same as G♭. We might be able to guess where F♭ is. So, go down by one semitone (fret) from F and we end up at the same place as the note as E! F♭ and E sound the same but have different names.

Finally, we have E, which was open. E♯ is rarely used but would be fret 1, the same as F. E♭ would be played on string 2, fret 4 as we can't get any lower on string 1!

JustinGUITAR

STRING 1
STRING 2
STRING 3
STRING 4
STRING 5
STRING 6
ACCIDENTALS
MORE RHYTHMS
SCALE STUDIES
REPERTOIRE

EXERCISE 40 *Accidentals*

STRING 1

STRING 2

STRING 3

STRING 4

STRING 5

STRING 6

ACCIDENTALS

MORE RHYTHMS

SCALE STUDIES

REPERTOIRE

STEP
41 | Accidentals on the thinnest three strings

This next exercise uses notes on the thinnest three strings. The rhythm is kept consistent because this exercise is all about the notes. It will help you get used to finding notes quickly, recognising the accidentals and how they affect the notes as soon as you can.

We already examined the notes on string 1, so let's have a brief look at string 2. The same principles apply, so hopefully it will make sense.

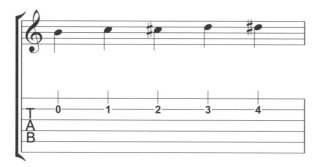

It's worth noting that, because of the tuning of the instruments, we have fewer possible accidentals to look at on string 3. Only G#/A♭ and A#/B♭. However, it's just as important of course!

You'll note that towards the end of the piece it gets quite intense. When there a lot of accidentals jumping around it's a real test of knowledge.

Don't forget that it's all just practice. This is a relatively new concept and bound to be tricky if you are not used to this kind of thing!

STRING 1

STRING 2

STRING 3

STRING 4

STRING 5

STRING 6

ACCIDENTALS

MORE RHYTHMS

SCALE STUDIES

REPERTOIRE

EXERCISE 41

Accidentals on the thinnest three strings

6

11

16

21

26

31

36

STRING 1

STRING 2

STRING 3

STRING 4

STRING 5

STRING 6

ACCIDENTALS

MORE RHYTHMS

SCALE STUDIES

REPERTOIRE

STEP 42 | Accidentals on all strings

Are you ready? We're now looking at accidentals on all 6 strings. This one is great for working on your note knowledge.

A good idea with this exercise is to take it in steps:

1. Play it through freely, taking your time and making sure you get all the notes right. Make sure everything makes sense and you know where the notes are. Take your time. Think. Learn. Understand.

2. Then play along with your metronome VERY slowly (40-50bpm). Try and get one note on each click. If you're finding that hard, try to get a note every 2 or 4 clicks. The key here is the regularity and feeling the pressure to find the note—it can really help!

Saying the notes out loud is also a great exercise. Both of us used to buy sheet music books and read them on the bus on the way to music college or before bed and we think it really helped. Recognising the note is one third of the journey and you can do it anywhere!

JustinGUITAR

STRING 1
STRING 2
STRING 3
STRING 4
STRING 5
STRING 6
ACCIDENTALS
MORE RHYTHMS
SCALE STUDIES
REPERTOIRE

EXERCISE 42 *Accidentals on all strings*

STRING 1

STRING 2

STRING 3

STRING 4

STRING 5

STRING 6

ACCIDENTALS

MORE RHYTHMS

SCALE STUDIES

REPERTOIRE

STEP

43 | Accidentals on all strings with rhythm

Now we will be introducing rhythm as well. When learning to read music, most people find this kind of exercise the hardest. Trying to internalise the rhythm while calculating the notes can do your head in! However, with slow and careful practice anybody can get there.

Doing it in steps can really help:

1. Name the notes without playing them.

2. Play through the exercise ignoring the rhythms, playing freely and pausing where needed.

3. Play through again now but keep the rhythm easy and consistent, slow but evenly spaced notes, with a metronome if you can!

4. Tap out the rhythm.

5. Try to play the whole thing in time!

We're getting a lot closer to 'real music' now. In fact, you will find a lot of sheet music that is easier than this—honestly!

This page is pretty tricky but that's the point of these kind of exercises. If you can handle this then when you see the odd accidental in a song it won't scare you.

EXERCISE
43

Accidentals on all strings with rhythm

STRING 1
STRING 2
STRING 3
STRING 4
STRING 5
STRING 6
ACCIDENTALS
MORE RHYTHMS
SCALE STUDIES
REPERTOIRE

STRING 1

STRING 2

STRING 3

STRING 4

STRING 5

STRING 6

ACCIDENTALS

MORE RHYTHMS

SCALE STUDIES

REPERTOIRE

STEP 44 | # All strings with accidentals, rhythms and rests

Now we will add rests in as well. Nothing is harder about this, you just have to include some silence! Counting along quietly in your head through rests is a really great idea, especially if they last any longer than a few beats.

Think of it as a chance to let your mind catch up as well.

Very good readers can 'read ahead', meaning they have notes ready to go in a kind of 'memory buffer', which gives them time to work out how to play any difficult passages, strange chords, difficult rhythms or work out the fingering.

At these early stages, we don't expect many of you will be able to read ahead, but bear in mind that good readers can do this, so allow yourself to look ahead a little if you can—but don't lose your place!

STRING 1

STRING 2

STRING 3

STRING 4

STRING 5

STRING 6

ACCIDENTALS

MORE RHYTHMS

SCALE STUDIES

REPERTOIRE

EXERCISE 44

All strings with accidentals, rhythms and rests

STRING 1

STRING 2

STRING 3

STRING 4

STRING 5

STRING 6

ACCIDENTALS

MORE RHYTHMS

SCALE STUDIES

REPERTOIRE

| STEP |
| 45 |

Accidentals, rhythms, rests and double-stops

Introducing accidentals to double-stops is a lethal combination as the amount of shapes possible grows to an astronomical amount. However, you will find that there are common combinations that you will see regularly and get to know. Unless you are playing avant-garde music, you are unlikely to come across double-stops where the two notes 'clash' harmonically.

As usual, take it slow, spend some time working it out and work your way up to playing the exercise as written. Don't be in a hurry, this is challenging stuff!

And don't forget that the accidentals affect the whole bar.

JustinGUITAR

STRING 1

STRING 2

STRING 3

STRING 4

STRING 5

STRING 6

ACCIDENTALS

MORE RHYTHMS

SCALE STUDIES

REPERTOIRE

EXERCISE
45 *Accidentals, rhythms, rests and double-stops*

STRING 1
STRING 2
STRING 3
STRING 4
STRING 5
STRING 6
ACCIDENTALS
MORE RHYTHMS
SCALE STUDIES
REPERTOIRE

STEP 46 — Chords and accidentals

This next exercise is designed to show you some of the common (and less common) chords that you might come across in open position.

Remember that the single notes are spelling the chord out for you, so pay attention to how you play them, knowing that at the end you will be playing the full chord.

STEP 47 — Duet #2

Duets are lovely to play and we can't recommend playing music with others highly enough, especially when learning to read. People make huge leaps and bounds playing duets when learning to read music. Perhaps it's not wanting to let your friend down, or some feeling of competition. However, the motivation or reason behind it isn't too important really—it just works.

If you don't have a jam buddy, record yourself, use a looper pedal, or play the parts one at a time as discussed earlier.

STRING 1
STRING 2
STRING 3
STRING 4
STRING 5
STRING 6
ACCIDENTALS
MORE RHYTHMS
SCALE STUDIES
REPERTOIRE

EXERCISE 46

Chords and accidentals

STRING 1

STRING 2

STRING 3

STRING 4

STRING 5

STRING 6

ACCIDENTALS

MORE RHYTHMS

SCALE STUDIES

REPERTOIRE

EXERCISE 47 *Duet #2*

STRING 1

STRING 2

STRING 3

STRING 4

STRING 5

STRING 6

STRING 1

STRING 2

STRING 3

STRING 4

STRING 5

STRING 6

ACCIDENTALS

MORE
RHYTHMS

SCALE
STUDIES

REPERTOIRE

| # Introduction to two voices

Classical guitar is a really great way to develop your reading. There is a lot of wonderful music to discover and it will really add a sense of refinement to your playing. Studying classical music will really help you to grow as a musician.

One thing you will often find in classical music is two 'voices' (two independent parts) written on one stave. You will be playing both parts at the same time so will essentially have twice as much information to process!

It might sound scary but it's nowhere near as bad as it might seem. In fact, we find it to be a lot of fun and we think you will too. It can be helpful to read through the two parts on their own before trying to play them together!

You will usually notice one line of notes with the stems pointing up (voice 1) and another with the stems pointing down (voice 2). Usually (but not always) the melody is played in voice 1 and the bass lines are played below in voice 2.

To play this type of exercise we recommend using finger-style. It's also possible using hybrid picking (pick and fingers) but it's a lot more challenging.

A general guideline regarding which finger to use:

- play the bass strings—the thickest 3 strings—using your thumb (this is normally written as voice 2)
- play notes on the G string with your index finger (voice 1)
- play notes on the B string with your middle finger (voice 1)
- play notes on the top E string with your ring finger (voice 1)

Check out the following exercise. Take it slowly, trying to get your head around reading two parts at once. As usual, you will find some things that pop up frequently that you will start to recognise right away. There will also be other new things, which might make you have to stop to figure out what is going on. Experienced readers nearly always have a 'read through' of a new piece first, looking for things that might stump them before even attempting to play it in time.

STRING 1
STRING 2
STRING 3
STRING 4
STRING 5
STRING 6
ACCIDENTALS
MORE RHYTHMS
SCALE STUDIES
REPERTOIRE

EXERCISE 48 *Introduction to two voices*

STRING 1

STRING 2

STRING 3

STRING 4

STRING 5

STRING 6

ACCIDENTALS

MORE RHYTHMS

SCALE STUDIES

REPERTOIRE

STEP 49 Introduction to syncopation

Next up we're going to be looking at rhythm in detail and specifically at something called syncopation. The common definition is 'a temporary displacement of the regular accent in music caused by stressing a weak beat'. In practice, it means putting notes on the 'ands' and not on the beat (numbers), which changes the pulse and flow of the music. It is very common and nothing to be scared of at all—just a new thing to get familiar with.

So, we're starting off with only quarter-notes and eighth-notes. Up until now we have always had notes starting on the beat (sometime rests) but never a succession of 'off beats'.

Some of the things we have included in this exercise are not things you will actually see (too complicated to explain the why and how here, so you'll have to believe us for now). However, you will find it very helpful to be able to read all these as you will encounter the 'wrong' ones from time to time (they're often quicker to write, but harder to read).

Take a look at the first bar of the exercise. Beats 1 and 2 look normal, but then we have an eighth-note followed by a quarter-note and another eighth-note (♪ ♩ ♪). You may have seen ♩ ♪ ♪ many times but this rhythmic combination means your notes will fall on the two 'ands' after beat 3. The second bar is the same figure, but placed at the beginning of the bar. This ♪ ♩ ♪ combination is very common and you need to get used to it.

Bar 3 introduces another level: an eighth-note followed by three quarter-notes and another eighth note. This should look quite unusual as you are used to seeing quarter-notes falling on the beat. However, that first eighth-note is pushing them all forward by half a beat, making a very syncopated rhythm. This is an unusual way to write this rhythm. It may even, sometimes, be considered wrong. The reason is that 'ties' (which we will study soon) can offer another way to write the same rhythm, making it much easier to read. Nevertheless it does come up in a reading situation so we thought we'd better include it.

Before you even think about adding notes to this, you should tap this one out a few times first as you are going to play some things that may feel confusing at first.

You might also like to try playing it all the way through just on one note, being sure to play the correct rhythm.

Only when you feel confident at tapping out the rhythm should you SLOWLY start to play it with notes as well.

Remember to start by counting '1 and 2 and 3 and 4 and' and keep it going ALL THE WAY THROUGH!

STRING 1
STRING 2
STRING 3
STRING 4
STRING 5
STRING 6
ACCIDENTALS
MORE RHYTHMS
SCALE STUDIES
REPERTOIRE

EXERCISE 49 *Introduction to syncopation*

STRING 1

STRING 2

STRING 3

STRING 4

STRING 5

STRING 6

ACCIDENTALS

MORE RHYTHMS

SCALE STUDIES

REPERTOIRE

STEP 50 — Eighth-note rests

You're about to make a new friend. Please allow me to introduce eighth-note rest! He looks like a '7' with a blob on the end and he's worth half a beat. So, two in a beat, eight in a bar of $\frac{4}{4}$.

Just to make a point, in bar 1 you'll see four eighth-note rests and two quarter-note rests. You should be completely silent for the duration of that bar. (This is clearly not the most efficient way to write a bar of silence but we wanted you to get used to those new rests.)

In bar 2 we have something interesting. An eighth-note followed by an eighth-note rest. The rhythm, if we were tapping it out, would be exactly the same as playing just four quarter-notes, but as shown, the second note will only be played for half of its value. This is important! The difference is in where the note ends.

In bar 3 we swap those two notes on beat 2 around so you have an eighth-note of silence followed by an eighth-note.

Often encountering these rhythms might feel like a giant step up in difficulty. The good news is that it doesn't last (for the vast majority of people). It's just a bit of a shocker when you first encounter them.

You should definitely spend a while tapping your way through this exercise before going anywhere near your guitar. We'll be developing these concepts more in a future book, but you should be aware of these concepts now because you will need them in the 'real world' if you want to start reading any piece of music.

Make sure you count along. Especially when you have a lot going on in a bar alongside unusual figures, you'll need to keep your wits about you (and count).

JustinGUITAR

STRING 1
STRING 2
STRING 3
STRING 4
STRING 5
STRING 6
ACCIDENTALS
MORE RHYTHMS
SCALE STUDIES
REPERTOIRE

EXERCISE 50 *Eighth-note rests*

STRING 1
STRING 2
STRING 3
STRING 4
STRING 5
STRING 6
ACCIDENTALS
MORE RHYTHMS
SCALE STUDIES
REPERTOIRE

STEP

51 Ties

Now we'll be introducing another new friend who you will get to know better in a later book but we'd like to introduce it to you now.

A tie very simply 'ties two notes together'. The most common question is 'why not write a longer note?' It's a fair question. The simplest answer is that there are only so many beats in bar and if you want a note to carry across the bar line you need a way of doing it. However, sometimes it makes it easier to read to use a tie as well.

Music should be written so it's easy to read. There are a number of tools that people use to make it easier. However, you will often encounter music that has not been written in the easiest way. It's worth getting familiar with every way you might see it.

In this exercise you can see that we start off staying on one note, making sure that you focus on the rhythm of the notes. However, remember you can also do this throughout the whole exercise as well.

The exercise takes you through many of the common ways that the tie will be used as well as some more unusual ones too. Just to make sure you get it, we've even combined them with some of the syncopated rhythms from the previous exercises.

We'll be looking at a lot more ties as we progress in future books. However, once again, get yourself familiar with the concept now and start developing a relationship with this new friend.

We looked at picking direction (down-strums and up-strums) during Step 23. However, we haven't looked at picking tied notes, so to avoid confusion we have included the picking directions for three lines on the next page. They follow the pattern of down-strokes on the beats and up-strokes on the 'ands'. This movement should never stop throughout the whole page. Having a basic system like this in place can make a tremendous difference in learning to play syncopated rhythms. Picking in the right direction helps with staying in time (much like the importance of keeping your hand moving when strumming).

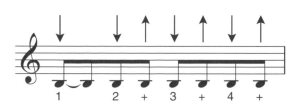

JustinGUITAR

STRING 1
STRING 2
STRING 3
STRING 4
STRING 5
STRING 6
ACCIDENTALS
MORE RHYTHMS
SCALE STUDIES
REPERTOIRE

EXERCISE 51 *Ties*

STRING 1

STRING 2

STRING 3

STRING 4

STRING 5

STRING 6

ACCIDENTALS

MORE RHYTHMS

SCALE STUDIES

REPERTOIRE

STEP
52 | Dots

One last new notation device to introduce you to is probably less common than syncopation and ties but you will see it very often. It's a small dot after a note, called a dot.

A dot after a note increases the note value by half of itself.

For instance, a half-note (normally worth two beats) when dotted is worth three beats (2 + 1).

$$\text{♩·} = 3$$

$$\text{♩} + \text{♩} = \text{♩·}$$

A quarter-note (normally worth 1 beat) when dotted is worth 1½ beats (1 + 0.5).

$$\text{♩·} = 1\frac{1}{2}$$

You can, of course, add dots to rests as well.

$$\text{𝄽·} = 1\frac{1}{2}$$

You can add dots to eighth-notes as well but that will be covered in a future book as it goes into smaller subdivisions than we cover in this volume.

STRING 1

STRING 2

STRING 3

STRING 4

STRING 5

STRING 6

ACCIDENTALS

MORE
RHYTHMS

SCALE
STUDIES

REPERTOIRE

EXERCISE 52 *Dots*

STRING 1

STRING 2

STRING 3

STRING 4

STRING 5

STRING 6

ACCIDENTALS

MORE RHYTHMS

SCALE STUDIES

REPERTOIRE

STEP
53 Introducing $\frac{6}{8}$ time

If you decide to explore some simple classical guitar music to help develop your reading (which we hope you will do) then you are likely to encounter other time signatures. $\frac{6}{8}$ is very common and has a very different feel to $\frac{4}{4}$.

$\frac{6}{8}$ time has six eighth-notes in a bar. Think about it: six-eighths. See why it's $\frac{6}{8}$? It is important to understand and feel that it is two groups of three notes. You will often see them grouped in threes.

What this means in practice is that you should feel and accent beats 1 and 4. A good way to get this feeling is to learn the counting for this time signature. It's one count for each eighth-note. Say '1, 2, 3, **4**, 5, 6' out loud, saying the 1 and 4 louder. Alternatively, you can tap it out on something and hit the 1 and 4 louder. Try to feel it. It kind of 'rolls' along. How does it make you feel?

Because the notes are commonly grouped in threes it means is that you will also see more dotted quarter-notes and rests (worth the equivalent of three eighth-notes) and more quarter-note/eighth-note combinations.

It's a lovely feel so don't be afraid of it. In fact I would recommend seeking out some easy $\frac{6}{8}$ pieces to have some fun with!

EXERCISE
53 *Introducing ⁶₈ time*

STRING 1
STRING 2
STRING 3
STRING 4
STRING 5
STRING 6
ACCIDENTALS
MORE RHYTHMS
SCALE STUDIES
REPERTOIRE

STEP 54 | $\frac{6}{8}$ Study

This $\frac{6}{8}$ study is a more musical example for you to explore. It contains many of the previous concepts including double-stops and rests.

EXERCISE
54
6/8 *Study*

STRING 1
STRING 2
STRING 3
STRING 4
STRING 5
STRING 6
ACCIDENTALS
MORE RHYTHMS
SCALE STUDIES
REPERTOIRE

STRING 1
STRING 2
STRING 3
STRING 4
STRING 5
STRING 6
ACCIDENTALS
MORE RHYTHMS
SCALE STUDIES
REPERTOIRE

STEP 55 | G major scale key study

We're going to introduce one more 'key' concept in this book: keys. We're not going too deeply into this as this isn't a theory book. For more information on how keys work please check out Justin's eBook, *Practical Music Theory (For Guitarists)*.

In the C major scale, there are no sharp or flat notes because the major scale formula specifies specific intervals between notes. The C major scale follows the formula (shown with T=Tone, S=Semitone) without needing sharps or flats:

However all other major keys have some sharps and flat in them, like G major for example:

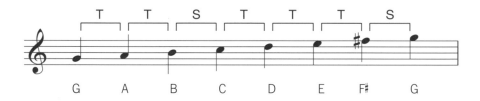

You can see from the above that the F was changed to an F♯ to make the scale notes fit the major scale formula. What this means in practice is that if you are playing a song in the key of G, when an F is played it will be an F♯ (unless a natural or flat sign precedes the F).

Rather than write an 'accidental' each time, it makes more sense to tell the reader that we're in the key of G and all the F notes will be played as F♯ unless shown otherwise. This is called a key signature and the F♯ will be shown at the beginning of the music. You'll see it after the clef but before the time signature.

Key signature for G major

There are many different keys and therefore key signatures. We'll be looking at just a few in this volume.

Have a go at the following exercise now and remember that every time you see the note F you will be playing it as an F♯ (one semitone above F in case you forgot).

It can be very helpful to learn the G major scale (shown at the start of the exercise) as this will help you remember where to put your fingers if there are no accidentals. One of the reasons people practise scales is to develop 'muscle memory' which can be very helpful when reading in different keys.

JustinGUITAR

STRING 1

STRING 2

STRING 3

STRING 4

STRING 5

STRING 6

ACCIDENTALS

MORE
RHYTHMS

SCALE
STUDIES

REPERTOIRE

EXERCISE
55

G major scale key study

STRING 1

STRING 2

STRING 3

STRING 4

STRING 5

STRING 6

ACCIDENTALS

MORE
RHYTHMS

SCALE
STUDIES

REPERTOIRE

STEP
56 F major scale key study

We've seen C major (no sharps or flats) and G major (with one sharp: F♯) so now it's time to look at a key with one flat: F major.

Here's a reminder of the C major scale, and the intervals between each consecutive note:

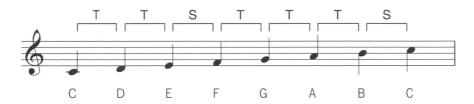

And here is the F major scale, which uses the same intervals but starts on the note F:

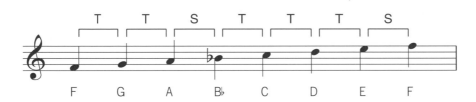

As you play this exercise you should play every B as a B♭ unless otherwise indicated by a natural sign.

As before, it is worth practicing the F major scale so that your fingers get used to the note placement on the fingerboard.

EXERCISE 56 — F major scale key study

STRING 1

STRING 2

STRING 3

STRING 4

STRING 5

STRING 6

ACCIDENTALS

MORE RHYTHMS

SCALE STUDIES

REPERTOIRE

STRING 1

STRING 2

STRING 3

STRING 4

STRING 5

STRING 6

ACCIDENTALS

MORE RHYTHMS

SCALE STUDIES

REPERTOIRE

STEP 57 D major scale key study

We've now looked at **C major** (no sharps or flats), **G major** (with one sharp: F♯) and **F major** (with one flat: B♭). Next we'll take a look at **D Major**, which has two sharps.

The C major scale:

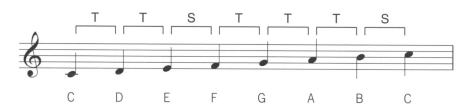

Below you can see the notes in the D major scale with the same formula as above.

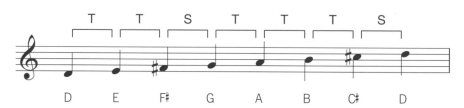

So, off you go again! This time remember to play every F and C as an F♯ and C♯ in all octaves, all the way through the exercise (unless shown to be different by another accidental).

STRING 1
STRING 2
STRING 3
STRING 4
STRING 5
STRING 6
ACCIDENTALS
MORE RHYTHMS
SCALE STUDIES
REPERTOIRE

EXERCISE 57

D major scale key study

STRING 1

STRING 2

STRING 3

STRING 4

STRING 5

STRING 6

ACCIDENTALS

MORE
RHYTHMS

SCALE
STUDIES

REPERTOIRE

STEP
58 | A major scale key study

We've seen **C major (no sharps or flats)**, **G major (with one sharp: F♯)**, **D Major (with two sharps: F♯ & C♯)** and **F major (with one flat: B♭)** and finally we're going to look at the key of A which has three sharps to remember!

The C major scale:

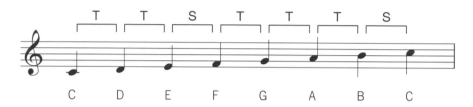

Below you can see the notes in the A Major scale with the formula above.

So off you go again - this time remember that every F, C and G will be played as an F♯, C♯ and G♯ respectively in all octaves, all the way through (unless shown to be different by another accidental).

STRING 1
STRING 2
STRING 3
STRING 4
STRING 5
STRING 6
ACCIDENTALS
MORE RHYTHMS
SCALE STUDIES
REPERTOIRE

EXERCISE
58 *A major scale key study*

STRING 1

STRING 2

STRING 3

STRING 4

STRING 5

STRING 6

ACCIDENTALS

MORE
RHYTHMS

SCALE
STUDIES

REPERTOIRE

STEP 59 Random note studies

As well as playing in different keys, doing random note studies can also be very effective in teaching you to recognise all the notes and helping you through any surprises you might encounter reading notated music.

As these studies are not usually melodically driven, they are usually more awkward to play. There are less 'natural' note choices and rhythms.

You will also encounter bigger jumps between notes. These might be more than you would expect in 'normal' music. If you can get used to these, then when you encounter the occasional big jumps or series of accidentals they will seem a little less scary.

EXERCISE
59 *Random note studies*

STRING 1

STRING 2

STRING 3

STRING 4

STRING 5

STRING 6

ACCIDENTALS

MORE RHYTHMS

SCALE STUDIES

REPERTOIRE

 # Repertoire

The last section of the book is for you to work on your reading because there is no substitute for just doing it! Seriously. If you want to become a good reader then you need to do it as much as you can. Devour everything you can find!

Remember that being able to read does not necessarily mean 'sight reading'. Often when reading a complex piece of music you will have to do it slowly and work out some of the chords, fingerings or, if not shown in the music, what position (area of the fingerboard) to play. 'Sight reading' really means to play on sight and is a very valuable skill but just being able to read slowly and figure it out is valuable as well.

Sight reading

If you are working on sight reading then you need as much new material as you can find—you should avoid memorising the music, as you are aiming to keep it fresh and having to work it out as you play.

You can use any music and just read it. Try reading any music you can find, even for other instruments. Flute music books are actually quite popular choices because the flute has a similar range but the phrasing is very different so it really encourages exploring where to play on the fretboard and figuring out position well in advance. Having said that, we're only looking at using the open position in this book.

Also remember that you can work on single elements of note reading. Just naming the notes out loud from a piano score will help you learn the names of the notes on the fretboard. But there is no substitute for real reading.

Learning music to perform or memorise

If you're studying a piece of guitar music to perform or learn by heart then you obviously want to remember it. The most effective way to learn a piece seems to be breaking it into chunks and then building up into the whole piece. It's a good idea to do it in stages:

Play through the piece a few times, sight reading as best you can just to get a feel for it and what the difficult parts might be. Do this very slowly, at 50% or less of the correct speed (unless it is super easy).

Work out which part of the fretboard you're in for each bit and check if there are any 'clues' (like string or finger indicators) in the music.

Start at the beginning, figure out the first bar and commit it to memory. Read it a few times, then look away and make sure it is still clear. Visualizing the music in your mind helps lock it in. The speed is not important here, only the notes and the correct rhythm are essential.

Once you are cool with bar 1, move onto bar 2 and work on that, and then join it on and make sure you have those two bars in your memory and that you can play them correctly—the right notes, the right rhythm and right fingers. But keep it slow.

Depending on the complexity of the piece this might actually be enough for one session. Just step away from it and do something else. Try recalling how these two bars go as often as you can. You don't need to spend much time thinking about them. Just recall the information often (3-5 times in a day). This is the most efficient way to learn.

STRING 1

STRING 2

STRING 3

STRING 4

STRING 5

STRING 6

ACCIDENTALS

MORE RHYTHMS

SCALE STUDIES

REPERTOIRE

JustinGUITAR

STRING 1
STRING 2
STRING 3
STRING 4
STRING 5
STRING 6
ACCIDENTALS
MORE RHYTHMS
SCALE STUDIES
REPERTOIRE

Continue like this all the way through until you have one section done. This might be the whole thing, or an 8- or 16-bar section of one piece depending on how long and/or complex it is.

Once you can play it all slowly try to play it all the way through with a slow metronome pulse and see which parts are difficult—work on those a bit extra. Try to be aware of how tense/relaxed you are as you're doing this. The problem is that we often tense up (press harder, do bigger movements, stop breathing, etc.) in the bars that worry us. The solution starts with being aware of that happening and consciously trying to relax during those difficult parts.

Slowly increase the tempo, each time looking for the difficult areas and returning to those after playing through to make sure that you are comfortable throughout the song. There will almost always be harder parts in pieces you learn and that is fine, but try to smooth it out as much as you can by working more on the harder sections.

Once you are confident playing it all the way through at a reasonable speed, start to notice dynamics (variations in the volume of the notes), tone (the way the notes sound) and tempo (where you might manipulate the tempo to help convey emotion).

Be aware of your feelings and emotions as you play. Try to get absorbed in the music, enjoy every note, every movement. This might seem a bit airy-fairy but we need to be in touch with our 'emotional' side if we are hoping to communicate something through our music.

Keep playing until you're ready to perform it!

Things to watch out for

We've included a range of different pieces here for you to explore—we have simplified some of the music a little (particularly the national anthems) so they fit with what we've looked at in the book so far, so please don't be offended if we slightly edited your country's national anthem!

Repeat Signs

A repeat barline looks like a thick line and a thin line and two dots. In the example below you will see the start repeat (with the dots on the right of the two lines) and the end repeat (with the dots on the left of the two lines). You will play right through a start repeat but when you get to the end repeat you will work your way backwards and start again from the first start repeat you come to. You can see it as eyes looking back and you start again at the first eyes you meet! Or like brackets. Just repeat what's inside the brackets.

1st and 2nd time bars

When a large section of music is to be repeated but the ending is different we use 1st and 2nd time bars. You'll see a long line above the music with a **1.** Just keep playing until you come across a repeat sign and go back to the start repeat (as described previously) and start playing again.

When you reach the **1.** (for the second time) you must now skip over it and play the line with a **2.** above it. Think of it like a gate that means you can only go in on certain visits!

In this example, the first time we finish bar 8, we then play the following bar with the **1.** above it, and repeat back to earlier in the piece. When we arrive at bar 9 for the second time, we jump straight over it, and play the bar with the **2.** above it, and carry on the piece from there.

Repertoire

01. Twinkle, Twinkle Little Star (key of C)
02. Frère Jacques (key of F)
03. Baa, Baa, Black Sheep (key of D)
04. Yankee Doodle (key of C)
05. Mary Had A Little Lamb (key of F)
06. Old MacDonald Had A Farm (key of G)
07. London Bridge Is Falling Down (key of C)
08. The Japanese National Anthem: 'Kimigayo' (key of F)
09. Jingle Bells (key of G)
10. Deck The Halls (key of F)
11. God Save The Queen (key of D)
12. A-Tisket, A-Tasket (key of C)
13. All Through The Night (key of G)
14. Scarborough Fair (key of F)
15. The Russian National Anthem (key of C)
16. I Saw Three Ships (key of G)
17. The Spanish National Anthem: 'Marcha Real' (key of A)
18. In The Bleak Midwinter (key of F)
19. The William Tell Overture (key of F)
20. Silent Night (key of C)
21. Advance Australia Fair (key of A)
22. We Three Kings (key of G)
23. Joy To The World (key of D)
24. The Italian National Anthem: 'Il Canto degli Italiani' (key of C)
25. The French Guitational Anthem: 'La Marseillaise' (key of C)
26. O Holy Night (key of C)
27. The Star-Spangled Banner (key of C)

REPERTOIRE 01 — *Twinkle, Twinkle Little Star (key of C)*

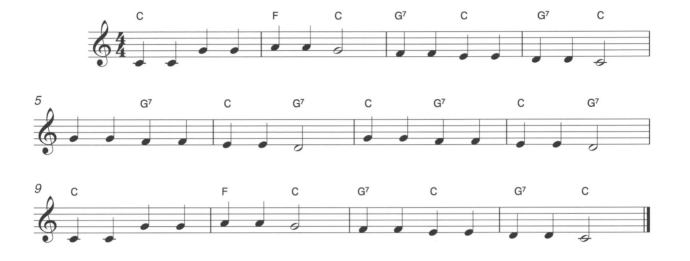

REPERTOIRE 02 — *Frère Jacques (key of F)*

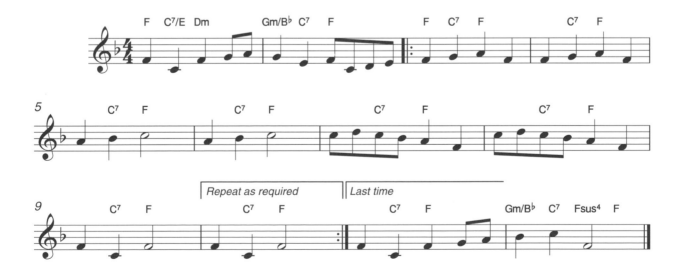

STRING 1
STRING 2
STRING 3
STRING 4
STRING 5
STRING 6
ACCIDENTALS
MORE RHYTHMS
SCALE STUDIES
REPERTOIRE

STRING 1

STRING 2

STRING 3

STRING 4

STRING 5

STRING 6

ACCIDENTALS

MORE RHYTHMS

SCALE STUDIES

REPERTOIRE

REPERTOIRE
03 *Baa, Baa, Black Sheep (key of D)*

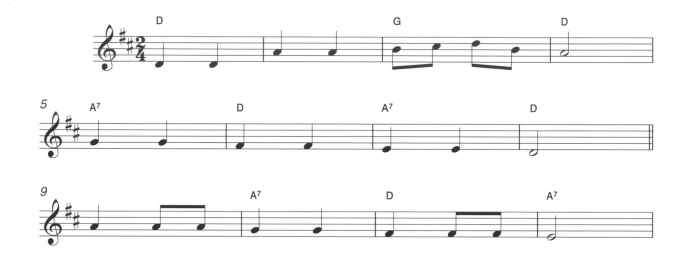

REPERTOIRE
04 *Yankee Doodle (key of C)*

JustinGUITAR

STRING 1
STRING 2
STRING 3
STRING 4
STRING 5
STRING 6
ACCIDENTALS
MORE RHYTHMS
SCALE STUDIES
REPERTOIRE

REPERTOIRE 05 — *Mary Had A Little Lamb (key of F)*

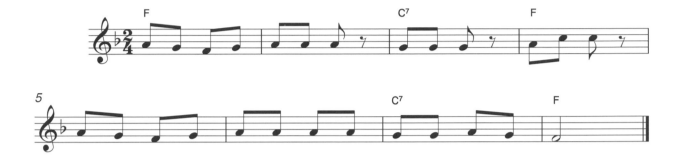

REPERTOIRE 06 — *Old MacDonald Had A Farm (key of G)*

STRING 1
STRING 2
STRING 3
STRING 4
STRING 5
STRING 6
ACCIDENTALS
MORE RHYTHMS
SCALE STUDIES
REPERTOIRE

REPERTOIRE 07

London Bridge Is Falling Down (key of C)

REPERTOIRE 08

The Japanese National Anthem: 'Kimigayo' (key of F)

REPERTOIRE

09 Jingle Bells (key of G)

STRING 1

STRING 2

STRING 3

STRING 4

STRING 5

STRING 6

ACCIDENTALS

MORE RHYTHMS

SCALE STUDIES

REPERTOIRE

REPERTOIRE
10   *Deck The Halls (key of F)*

JustinGUITAR

STRING 1
STRING 2
STRING 3
STRING 4
STRING 5
STRING 6
ACCIDENTALS
MORE RHYTHMS
SCALE STUDIES
REPERTOIRE

REPERTOIRE 11 *God Save The Queen (key of D)*

STRING 1

STRING 2

STRING 3

STRING 4

STRING 5

STRING 6

ACCIDENTALS

MORE RHYTHMS

SCALE STUDIES

REPERTOIRE

REPERTOIRE 12

A-Tisket, A-Tasket (key of C)

REPERTOIRE 13

All Through The Night (key of G)

JustinGUITAR

STRING 1
STRING 2
STRING 3
STRING 4
STRING 5
STRING 6
ACCIDENTALS
MORE RHYTHMS
SCALE STUDIES
REPERTOIRE

REPERTOIRE 14 *Scarborough Fair (key of F)*

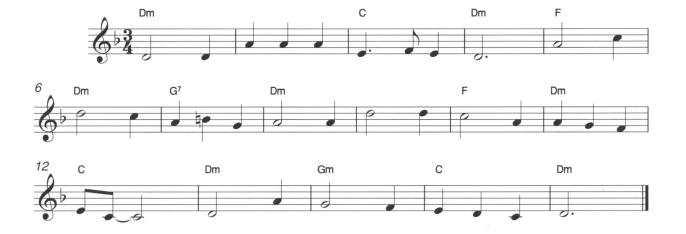

REPERTOIRE 15 *The Russian National Anthem (key of C)*

STRING 1
STRING 2
STRING 3
STRING 4
STRING 5
STRING 6
ACCIDENTALS
MORE RHYTHMS
SCALE STUDIES
REPERTOIRE

REPERTOIRE
16   *I Saw Three Ships (key of G)*

REPERTOIRE
17   *The Spanish National Anthem: 'Marcha Real' (key of A)*

JustinGUITAR

STRING 1
STRING 2
STRING 3
STRING 4
STRING 5
STRING 6
ACCIDENTALS
MORE RHYTHMS
SCALE STUDIES
REPERTOIRE

REPERTOIRE 18 *In The Bleak Midwinter (key of F)*

STRING 1

STRING 2

STRING 3

STRING 4

STRING 5

STRING 6

ACCIDENTALS

MORE RHYTHMS

SCALE STUDIES

REPERTOIRE

REPERTOIRE 19 *The William Tell Overture (key of F)*

STRING 1

STRING 2

STRING 3

STRING 4

STRING 5

STRING 6

ACCIDENTALS

MORE RHYTHMS

SCALE STUDIES

REPERTOIRE

REPERTOIRE 20 — *Silent Night (key of C)*

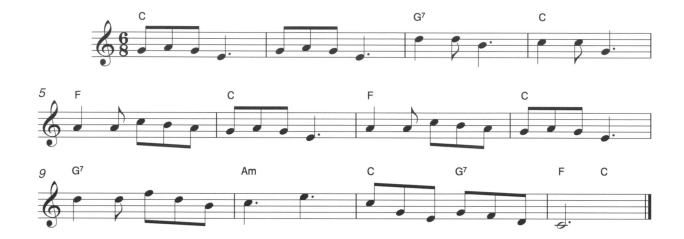

REPERTOIRE 21 — *Advance Australia Fair (key of A)*

JustinGUITAR

STRING 1

STRING 2

STRING 3

STRING 4

STRING 5

STRING 6

ACCIDENTALS

MORE RHYTHMS

SCALE STUDIES

REPERTOIRE

REPERTOIRE
22 *We Three Kings (key of G)*

STRING 1

STRING 2

STRING 3

STRING 4

STRING 5

STRING 6

ACCIDENTALS

MORE RHYTHMS

SCALE STUDIES

REPERTOIRE

REPERTOIRE 23 *Joy To The World (key of D)*

REPERTOIRE 24

The Italian National Anthem: 'Il Canto degli Italiani' (key of C)

JustinGUITAR

STRING 1
STRING 2
STRING 3
STRING 4
STRING 5
STRING 6
ACCIDENTALS
MORE RHYTHMS
SCALE STUDIES
REPERTOIRE

STRING 1
STRING 2
STRING 3
STRING 4
STRING 5
STRING 6
ACCIDENTALS
MORE RHYTHMS
SCALE STUDIES
REPERTOIRE

The Italian National Anthem (continued)

5th fret, top E string

JustinGUITAR

STRING 1

STRING 2

STRING 3

STRING 4

STRING 5

STRING 6

ACCIDENTALS

MORE RHYTHMS

SCALE STUDIES

REPERTOIRE

REPERTOIRE 25

The French National Anthem: 'La Marseillaise' (key of C)

STRING 1

STRING 2

STRING 3

STRING 4

STRING 5

STRING 6

ACCIDENTALS

MORE RHYTHMS

SCALE STUDIES

REPERTOIRE

REPERTOIRE 26 *O Holy Night (key of C)*

JustinGUITAR

STRING 1

STRING 2

STRING 3

STRING 4

STRING 5

STRING 6

ACCIDENTALS

MORE RHYTHMS

SCALE STUDIES

REPERTOIRE

REPERTOIRE 27 *The Star-Spangled Banner (key of C)*